THE
DIY POCKET
BIBLE

THE
DIY POCKET
BIBLE

STEPHEN GILES

PB POCKET BIBLES

This edition first published in Great Britain 2009 by
Crimson Publishing, a division of Crimson Business Ltd
Westminster House
Kew Road
Richmond
Surrey
TW9 2ND

A catalogue record for this book is available from the British Library.

ISBN 978 1 907087 06 6

Disclaimer Note: The material contained in this book is set out in good
faith for general guidance and no liability can be accepted for loss, injury or
expense incurred as a result of relying in particular circumstances or state-
ments made in this book.

Typeset by RefineCatch Ltd, Bungay, Suffolk

Printed and bound by LegoPrint SpA, Trento

CONTENTS

ACKNOWLEDGEMENTS

I would like to thank the following DIY experts for their help, support and advice in the preparation of this book: Steve Edwards, Barry Giles, Andy Simmonds, Ian Mather and John Rogers. Without their insight, wisdom and experience it would have been a DIY nightmare.

I would also like to thank Lucy Edwards for her great help, Sarah for patience and tea, and Beth at Crimson for letting me loose on it in the first place.

INTRODUCTION

There's a huge range of DIY jobs that anyone can do with a bit of forethought, the right tools and guidance. You might never have considered yourself as having a natural aptitude for DIY, but unless you're wealthy enough to summon up an expert every time a wall needs touching up or a washer needs replacing, anyone with their own home and an eye on their budget needs to know what to do and how to do it right.

DIY isn't just first aid for your house. With a basic understanding of plumbing, carpentry and decorating, you can convert a room, transform a living space, maybe even ultimately tackle larger and more demanding jobs, such as refurbishing a kitchen or bath-room. The number of websites, TV shows, magazines and other materials available all point to the fact that DIY is not just essential, it's also fun, rewarding and ultimately downright useful.

If you want evidence of the unflagging popularity of DIY as a leisure pursuit, take a look at the statistics provided in the Office for National Statistics 2009 social trends survey. A staggering 46% of men and 26% of women listed DIY as a pastime they enjoyed. Only shopping and watching TV rank higher for both sexes and the chances are most of those people are shopping in DIY ware-houses or watching makeover TV shows.

Recessions and times of austerity always encourage people to get off their seats and flex their creative muscles. DIY was born in the post-war era when everyone wanted to make the world around them just a little bit better.

In this book you'll find guidance on a range of projects, trouble-shooting, installation advice, buying guides, safety hints and a whole host of top tips, rules of thumb and some golden rules of DIY that will guide you along this well-trodden path.

In this book we start with the basics and some common problems and then work through projects with varying degrees of complexity until we get to the jobs that simply can't be handled alone. Then we come to the question: to GABI or not to GABI?

'Getting A Bloke In' (GABI) is something we all have to do at some stage. Even the most talented DIY expert isn't likely to be able to manage every single aspect of a job, so there's no shame in getting on the phone to someone who has years of experience and the right tools for the job.

The DIY Pocket Bible collects together a huge variety of advice and guidance to give you a handy instant reference for all but the most specialist jobs around the home – so enjoy reading, work safely and take it steady.

Did you know?

The phrase DIY first came into popular usage in 1950s America. The USA is now the home of an 'extreme' form of the pastime, known colloquially as 'DEY', or Do Everything Yourself. We're not quite ready for that yet . . .

NOTE TO READERS

The length, width, weight and diameter of most DIY materials are calculated using the metric scale. Lengths are given in metres or millimetres (1,000mm to a metre). See p. 127 for a conversion table.

COMMON PROBLEMS AND HOW TO FIX THEM

⚒ BEFORE YOU BEGIN ⚒

DIY Golden Rule No. 1 ⚡

Before you start anything, stop, check your plan, rest and check again. Never rush a DIY job. Sometimes the difference between success and disaster is a cup of tea and a think.

PREPARATION

This chapter deals with the essentials of doing anything yourself – effectively this part of the book is DIY 101 and it should provide you with the answer to many of the emergencies that you could realistically expect to fix by yourself.

Rule one of house maintenance is to be prepared and have the right tools for the job. But before you even start, there's some very important groundwork to do.

1. **Know your enemy.** The most serious DIY-related problems involve water, electricity or gas (and sometimes all three). Problems involving any of these will require the isolation of the

problem as a first step. In the case of electricity this means turning off the mains power. Gas and water can be turned off with a stop cock or valve. The gas stop cock will be located near the gas meter and the water stop cock is normally found under the kitchen sink or possibly in the road outside the house. In all cases it is essential to locate the isolation switch before you do any work.

2. **Make a plan.** Once you've identified the sources of isolation, make a plan of your house with these clearly marked. Include any stop valves that lead from your cold water tank in the loft, and isolator valves for sink and bath taps. In an ideal world you will also have a plan of the electrical circuit of your house so that you know where mains cables run, but that may be impractical. Put this plan and essential emergency phone numbers (gas, electric, water) in a safe, easily accessible place with a good, powerful torch and spare batteries and make sure everyone in your house knows where it is.

Get tooled up

Before you do anything, you need to assemble a basic toolkit. Countless hours are wasted – and expensive mistakes are made – by people attempting a DIY job with an incorrect or inappropriate tool. Opinion is divided on what constitutes the 'ideal' basic toolkit and obviously the tools you choose will be determined in part by the jobs you tackle, but as a rule you shouldn't start anything without the following, which are all available from any good DIY store or hardware retailer:

- **Metal stud/pipe detector/cable locator.** This really is a necessary piece of kit (cost £10–£20) if you want to avoid the incredible inconvenience of putting a nail/screw through a pipe or wire.

- **Cordless drill.** Choose something that will cut through masonry, metal and wood, with a power rating of 9v–18v and hammer action. If you're going to use the drill regularly, spend a few extra pounds on a recognised brand – it will pay for itself in time. A cheaper brand will be fine if you're only planning to put up the occasional set of shelves. Finally, make sure you get a drill with a lithium ion battery pack, as they have no charging 'memory', which means they can be recharged at will without affecting the life of the battery. If you're drilling lots of brick or concrete, get an SDS drill, which is a type of pneumatic drill that's much more effective for high-impact work. A cheap one will cost you less than £50. Also, don't forget to factor in the cost of decent-quality drill bits for wood and masonry, as cheaper drills (even those from good manufacturers) won't include bits as part of the package. This can add £15–£20 to the cost of your purchase (cost for cordless drill £40–£80+).

- **Quality adjustable spanner.** Combination spanners are useful when you're working with nuts and bolts in easily accessible areas, but for sheer versatility nothing beats a high-quality adjustable spanner – especially when dealing with plumbing jobs in hard-to-reach places. Buy the best quality you can afford – an alloy of chrome and steel or chrome and vanadium is the best choice (cost £10–£15).

- **Safety kit.** All serious DIY enthusiasts should ensure they are well equipped with safety gear. Think about safety from head to toe – from eye protection when drilling, hammering or sanding to toe protection (steel-toed boots) when lifting and carrying. Gripper gloves, which look like gardening gloves with little rubber studs on, are great for carrying or holding heavy or slippery items. These are especially good for anywhere you want to protect your hands and give yourself safe grip – again a very useful aid in a plumbing job. If you're dealing with dirty or unhygienic conditions, then PVC or latex gloves are good for single use. For more tips on DIY safety, see Chapter 5.

- **Tenon saw and panel saw.** These are the essential handsaws – if you're cutting a lot of metal pipes you'll also need a decent quality hacksaw. The tenon saw is perfect for small-scale cutting and detail work, the panel saw for rougher cuts of timber. Buy reasonable quality, but do be prepared to renew your saws when they become blunt.

- **Chisels (6mm and 20mm).** A couple of decent chisels should help you with most basic woodworking jobs. Quality is important – a strong metal chisel will last for years and will tolerate repeated sharpening.

- **Screwdrivers.** A decent set of screwdrivers is essential – there's nothing worse than using the wrong-sized driver, which damages the head of a screw and ultimately causes much headache. Select your drivers carefully to give the maximum reach across a range of sizes and situations. Stubby screwdrivers and long-handled screwdrivers are both useful for hard-to-reach jobs. Make sure you have a selection of crosshead and flat-head drivers.

- **Mallet and one-piece forged claw hammer.** The first of these is a universally useful tool when it comes to taking the gentle approach to demolition. It's the perfect tool for chipping away at masonry or plasterwork, but shouldn't be used for nailing. The claw hammer is a woodworking tool and needs to be strong enough to effectively remove nails as well. Try a few hammers for size, as weight and grip comfort are important factors in your choice.

- **Set square, measuring tape, spirit level.** These are all essential elements of preparation. The set square is a marking tool for wood, especially useful when trying to get joints square and accurate. The measuring tape, or laser measure, and spirit level (or laser level) are brilliant time-savers for tiling, shelving and woodworking. There are ways to circumvent these tools, but they're such an integral part of the success of a job, you'd be foolish to start without them.

- **Workbench**. You don't need a permanent bench for DIY, but you do need a flat, clear surface that you can use to safely balance and secure the item you're working on. In an ideal world that means a good quality 'work-mate' style folding bench. These are light yet safe and don't take up too much space, allowing you to work around the house without mess, fuss and danger. Again, get the best you can afford, but you won't break the bank — basic models are around £35–£50.

Pocket tip 🔨

Always keep your tools clean and your blades sharp. It will require less effort and you're less likely to injure yourself because you were pushing too hard with a blunt chisel. Good-quality saws should be sharpened by a specialist saw doctor, whereas cheaper saws are more or less disposable and should be replaced when blunt. You can sharpen your own chisels or screwdrivers on a whetstone (a hard sharpening stone that occurs naturally but is most commonly sold as a man-made ceramic compound). You can buy a whetstone from any good DIY store.

In addition to your basic toolkit, you'll also need something to store it in. Once again, opinion is divided as to the best options, but most professionals prefer a soft, wide-opening canvas bag. Tools are all pretty robust, so the idea that you need a huge plastic or steel strong-box for them is a bit of a myth. If a tool bag was good enough for your grandfather, it's good enough for you.

Drills – a guide

Your drill is one of the most important bits of kit you'll need and there's a whole range of technical options when choosing the drill. Your choice will depend on type of use, frequency of use and budget, but here are some of the key terms explained:

Torque: *This can be defined as turning force. Larger, more versatile drills have a greater range of speed settings, allowing them to be used at high and low torque. Low torque is useful for putting in screws or when starting a hole when you want low force.*

Chuck: *This is the 'mouth' of the drill, where the bit rests. Chucks are either keyed – ie requiring a short, fat cog-like key to open and close the jaw of the chuck – or keyless. The latter type opens by twisting the chuck mounting. This type is easier and faster.*

Variable speed setting: *Good drills have at least two speed settings. If you want to use a drill as a screwdriver, choose one with variable speed options.*

Hammer action: *Particularly useful for cutting into tough materials such as brickwork and masonry, hammer drills* *actually force the chuck and bit back and forth to drive them into the stonework. Hammer drills are more prone to wearing out than other types. Also, be sure to use the correct drill bit or you'll just destroy a weak bit and ruin your job.*

Reverse drive: *Another essential feature for screwdrivers, this allows you to remove screws.*

Handle: *More powerful drills, especially those that require a degree of user pressure, come with an extra handle at right angles to the trigger handle on the drill. This gives extra purchase and helps you drive into tough materials.*

There are plenty of other tools that you'll need, depending on the job – mentioned in the specific projects – but the above will give you a solid base to build from.

When it comes to specialist tools for one-off jobs, such as floor sanders, cement mixers and wood-flooring nailers, your best bet is to hire the equipment from a reputable hire shop (such as www.hss.com). As well as providing you with the latest kit in fully serviced condition, they will also advise you on safe handling of equipment and may even provide some safety kit as standard.

'If you want a thing done well, do it yourself.'
Napoleon Hill

If you can't find the right tool at the right time

Can't find a funnel? Use a roll of newspaper.

Can't find a scraper? Use a large bulldog clip.

Can't get lumps, grit and dust out of paint? Strain it through some tights.

Can't find a lubricant? Use cooking oil, soap or butter.

Can't find tile spacers? Use uncooked spaghetti.

Can't find a wall plug? Spent matches offer a quick fix.

Can't find the protective sleeve for your handsaw? Use a split piece of rubber hose.

⊶ PLUMBING ⊶

Before you tackle any plumbing repair, first isolate the water supply. The internal stop valve is normally found under the kitchen sink. If you can't turn off the stop valve having used reasonable force, go out in the street and turn off the stopcock in the street at the point where the supply enters your house. If your property is metered, you may well find the exterior stopcock in the same place as the meter.

Pocket tip ↖

Turning off the exterior stopcock will generally isolate only your supply, but older houses may share a supply, so check with your neighbours to make sure you've not cut off their water as well.

You should also check valves on supply from storage tanks in the roof and service valves on cisterns and taps – and do make sure any valves work **before** you need them.

Remember that even if you've turned the stopcock off you can still have 50 litres to 100 litres of water in a tank in your roof space that's going to come out and flood your house – so make sure that is isolated too.

Rule of thumb ↖

Don't forget to reinstate the positions of the valves at the end of any plumbing job; otherwise you could cause severe damage to your heating system.

WHAT TO DO . . .

IF YOU NAIL OR SCREW THROUGH A WATER PIPE

Don't panic – and don't remove the nail or screw. In the short term it is limiting the flow of the leak and is better off where it is. If you *have* removed the nail or screw, put it back in. The next step is to turn off the water supply at the stop cock/valve. If the pipe is part of your central heating system, turn this off as well – especially if you have a combination boiler – otherwise you'll find your house flooded by hot water.

Drain the system by turning your cold water taps on full. When the system is empty you need to replace the damaged section of pipe. That might not be an immediate possibility so you also need to know how to make a temporary fix.

The three most realistic options for a quick fix are the following:

1. Use a short section of garden hose or similar rubberised pipe split along one side, then bind to the damaged water pipe using hose clips (such as the Jubilee Clips brand).

2. Use an epoxy filler to bind the damaged area – this is normally found in the plumbing section of larger DIY stores.

3. Use a specialist pipe clamp. These are available from plumbing suppliers, and can be fixed to the damaged pipe with screws.

The only safe longer-term option for the repair is to remove the damaged section of pipe. Cut the pipe out with a **hacksaw** and replace with a new section using pressure fittings.

Pocket tip 🔨

To avoid nailing or screwing into water pipes that run under the floorboards of your house, draw a map of the pipe network on the floorboards themselves using a thick marker pen (if you're not going for sanded wooden floors).

IF WATER IS COMING THROUGH A CEILING

The cause of this problem is likely to be leaking or damaged pipes – which ultimately means following the procedures outlined above to repair. But in the interim you've got ceiling damage and a lot of excess water to deal with.

- If you've just got a small leak, stick a drawing pin into the ceiling below to make a fine hole, which will allow the water to drip through in a controlled manner.

- If the leak is more serious and the ceiling plaster is beginning to bulge, resist the temptation to slash the hole to relieve the pressure – sticking a knife, or a finger, into the centre of the bulge will bring the whole lot down in one extremely expensive mass of congealed plaster.

- Assuming you've turned off the water and the heating system, you should also switch off the electricity at the mains as a lot of electrical cables and junctions will be inside the void between floors. Then grab a torch and a cordless drill with a ¼ inch drill bit and drill half a dozen holes in the area of the leak. Once the water is collected, you can repair both the pipe and ceiling.

Pocket tip ✎

You might want to wear a raincoat and place some buckets and waterproof sheets underneath the leak as it can come through quite fast.

IF YOUR OVERFLOW IS OVERFLOWING

The likely cause of this is a stuck or damaged valve in the cold water header tank or in your toilet cistern. There are two types of valves used in loft tanks:

- piston valves
- diaphragm valves.

Diaphragm valves are standard on all new installations, but you may still have an old piston type. Diaphragm valves are usually plastic and won't fail or cause too many problems; piston valves can sometimes clog up with limescale or wear out through repeated use.

Isolate the water supply, remove the piston valve and replace with a diaphragm valve. These are fairly easy to install as a like-for-like replacement and can be purchased from plumbing supply shops and large DIY retailers.

Pocket tip ✎

Leaking ball valves can be caused by corrosion joining the slide mechanism, which may be corrected by pushing the float up and down a few times.

The float in your cistern or header tank may also be the cause of the problem – especially if it's an old metal type, as these can spring leaks and fill with water. Replace with a plastic float and this should fix the problem.

Pocket tip ↖

If you need to waterproof a damaged metal float temporarily, tie a small plastic bag (such as a sandwich bag) around the float.

IF A RADIATOR IS LEAKING

In most cases, leaks in radiators occur around joints. These are caused by corrosion in the system and the only long-term solution is to replace the system or the radiator.

To remove and replace a radiator:

● Make sure the central heating system is switched off.

● Close the valves at either end of the radiator you are removing and place large trays to catch the water under each valve.

● Keep a large plastic bowl standing by to empty the contents of the radiator into.

● Protect the surrounding walls and paintwork with some old plastic sheets, as the water will be black and grimy.

● Keeping a firm grip on the valve pipe work so you don't bend it, undo the coupling nuts to let the water come out, but don't remove them completely.

● Once most of the water has drained from the radiator, completely undo the coupling nuts and take the radiator off its wall brackets and empty the residue into the bowl.

If the leak isn't serious and you don't want to replace the radiator – for example, if you've got an old cast-iron radiator that you'll struggle to find a match for – you can put a leak-inhibiting substance into the header tank or into the radiator itself through the bleed valve.

These proprietary products are made by companies such as Fernox, and they pass small particles harmlessly around your system, but when they find a leak they work like blood clots, finding a hole and gradually setting solid. Although this isn't a permanent fix, it will work over the medium term. This kind of repair is especially good for weeping joints.

Pocket tip ↖

Use softened chewing gum as a short-term leak fix around a joint. It won't hold for long, but it may just save your carpet from a nasty black stain.

IF A TAP IS DRIPPING OR LEAKING

Pocket tip ↖

Before you begin any work around sinks, baths or drains, protect the ceramic or steel surface from falling spanners with a towel and put the plug in to stop screws, nuts and washers disappearing down the plughole.

There are a few reasons why a tap might be dripping or leaking – and the source of the leak will give you a clue as to the problem.

● The first possibility is that the washer on the tap has failed. This will show itself in a leak at the bottom of the tap's handle section. Turn off the water supply, empty the pipe of water and remove the head of the tap, replace the washer, use a little oil or WD-40 to lubricate and then reattach.

Pocket tip ↖

If you don't have the correct size of replacement washer, you can make a temporary repair by turning a worn washer over. Replace this as soon as you've got the right spare.

- The second likely source of a leak is the O-ring or packing gland around the spindle of the tap (an O-ring is the more modern variant). This shows itself as a leak from the top of the tap handle. A leak doesn't necessarily mean you need to replace the ring; it may just require a tightening of the gland nut, which sits on top of the headgear (the main part of the handle mechanism). If this doesn't correct the leak, try dismantling the tap mechanism and replacing the ring.

Rule of thumb ↘

As with all plumbing jobs involving sealed joints, it's a good idea to wrap thin strands of PTFE tape (available from plumbing suppliers) around the joint to ensure a watertight finish.

IF YOU HAVE A BLOCKAGE

Wastewater plumbing requires u-bends to trap smells and ensure they don't back up into the house, but this roller-coaster ride of discharge is prone to blockage. This is unavoidable, but if the blockage builds up, you could have a serious plumbing job on your hands. So, the answer is early identification and eradication. Blockages occur in three main areas:

Sink wastes. Kitchen sinks are especially vulnerable to blockages from food waste or fat.

- In the first instance these can be cleared by using a household drain cleaner – though these are only useful if there's no standing water.

- Otherwise, bale out the excess water and try using washing soda and boiling water.

- If the blockage is caused by solidified fat, gently heat the waste trap with a hairdryer.

- For more stubborn blockages, you may need to use a plunger or remove the waste pipe trap altogether so as to clear it out properly.

- Remember, if you have to take the waste pipe trap off, it will be full of water (don't be tempted to empty it down the sink!), so keep a bucket handy.

Pocket tip ↖

Washing soda and water, mixed with a little vinegar, also dissolves hair blockages in shower and bathroom sink drain blockages.

Toilet blockages. These are commonly caused when someone's put something unsuitable down the pan. The best, non-chemical options are plunging and rodding with a 'plumber's snake' – a metal spiral that works like mini drain rods.

Exterior drain blockages. The best tool for this job is drain rods. You can hire them cheaply, but you might be better off buying them if you have troublesome drains. Make sure you get a corkscrew and plunger attachment with the rods. Once you've removed the drain cover, feed the rods slowly into the drain, firmly adding sections one at a time and trying not to twist the rods too much. Push with the 'plunger' rod until you dislodge the blockage, or pull the obstruction back with the corkscrew.

Rule of thumb 🖎

When reconnecting waste pipes, smear some Vaseline around the rubber seals. This makes them slide and bed in easily.

IF YOUR SYSTEM IS MAKING A NOISE

Sometimes noise in the system is caused by air bubbles hitting the blades of the pump. A lack of pressure can also be a problem – a boiler running at low pressure will make more noise because the air bubbles are allowed to expand in the heating chamber of the boiler. You can check the pressure on a gauge on your boiler. The system should operate at a pressure level of around 2bar. If the pressure drops below 1.5bar, top it up by turning the valve below the boiler. You can also purchase additives that will reduce boiler noise.

Pocket tip 🖎

Think simple – remove air bubbles from your central heating system by bleeding radiators regularly with a bleed key. Don't forget to hold a piece of rag or kitchen towel beneath the bleed key as you turn the radiator valve. Water in your central heating system is black and can easily stain floors and paintwork.

IF YOU SMELL GAS

If you smell gas don't touch anything, don't turn any electrical items on and don't use your mobile phone or your landline. If the lights are on, leave them on. Make sure everyone leaves the house as soon as possible, then get to a safe distance and phone the gas emergency helpline on your mobile.

Before you get too far away you could try turning your gas off at the main meter (if it's outside). You could also open the windows and doors, but again, the safest option is to **get out and stay out** – if you do need to re-enter the building, make sure you do so alone and don't take your phone in with you – anything that creates a spark will potentially cause an explosion.

Emergency number for gas leaks throughout the UK, operated by the National Grid: **0800 111 999**

> 'Belief in oneself is one if the most important bricks in building any successful venture.'
> *Lydia M. Child*

⊷ CARPENTRY ⊷

WHAT TO DO . . .

IF A WOODEN DOOR OR WINDOW FRAME WON'T SHUT OR LOCK

External timber doors and windows expand and contract because of seasonal changes, or because of a lack of preparation – ie they haven't been painted or varnished properly and moisture is seeping into the wood.

- Provided the frame hasn't rotted, you need to dry out the affected area. You could wait for a period of dry weather or you could draw out the moisture with a hairdryer.

- Then plane or sand down the affected area and seal it properly by painting or varnishing with an exterior-grade product.

- Don't forget to paint or seal the underside of the door or window frame.

Pocket tip 🔨

Waxing sash windows helps them slide more smoothly.

Interior doors sometimes slip on their hinges, causing them to stick or the lock to fail. Don't be tempted to relocate the striking plate (the ironmongery on the frame where the lock engages) as this will just leave you with a badly fitting door prone to draughts. Remove the door and refit the hinges – you may need to add some thin strips of packing behind the hinges to give better support – or even add a third hinge to the frame to improve the structural strength.

Rule of thumb 🔨

Add a third hinge as a matter of course to any door that is exposed to moisture changes — this includes front and back doors, kitchen doors and bathroom doors.

Pocket tip 🔨

If a lock doesn't turn, some light oil will help. Oiling will also help if the tongue of the latch is tight.

IF YOU BREAK A WOOD-FRAMED WINDOW

Step one is be careful, not simply because of the broken glass you're coming into contact with, but also because if your broken window is upstairs or overlooks a road, you may cause real danger to passers-by unless you take precautions.

● First, tape up the window with masking tape, or even better use thick parcel tape to bind together the big shards.

● Then, using thick gloves, remove any large pieces of glass. Knock out the remaining glass and putty from the window frame using a hammer and cold chisel. Remember to work carefully around the frame itself.

● Once the old glass and putty has been removed, place a new line of putty around the frame, sit your new piece of glass inside the frame and then nail in tacks to hold the glass securely before adding more putty to finish off.

Rule of thumb

All replacement glass in windows and doors should be tough-ened safety glass, regardless of the thickness of the pane it is replacing.

IF YOU HAVE A CREAKY FLOORBOARD

Creaky floorboards are normally caused by nails rising up in the corners of boards.

- Using a claw hammer or pliers, lift out the nails and replace them with screws, which will hold fast in any conditions.

- If you want to make absolutely sure that the board is fixed tight, add more screws, but remember to check beneath the board for pipe work or cables.

If the floorboards are uneven or poor quality, you can reduce the risk of creating pressure points and produce a smooth overall fin-ish for a carpeted room by screwing a quarter-inch-thick covering of plywood across the entire surface of the floor. This will spread the weight of any downward pressure on individual boards and may reduce problems with squeaking.

Pocket tip

Working candle wax into the joint between floorboards can stop them creaking. On stairs, pouring PVA glue into the joints and leaving it to set overnight will eliminate squeaks.

⟞⟞ ELECTRICITY ⟞⟞

WHAT TO DO . . .

IF A FUSE BLOWS

The fuse box is the heart of your electrical system and even if you don't want to deal with electricity issues yourself, it pays to know what type of system you have and how it operates.

There are three main types of fuse box:

1. **Removable wire fuses.** The most old-fashioned type of fuse box, increasingly rare and fairly dangerous. Each circuit of your house (lighting, ring main, high-power appliances – such as a shower or immersion) has a different capacity of fuse wire depending on the amount of current required. Lighting requires a five-amp fuse, ring mains need 30-amp wire and others may require a 15-amp – check the appliance you are using to ensure the correct fuse.

2. **Cartridge fuses.** These are a more modern version of the above. They're easier to use because there's no need to cut wires, but it's harder to detect a fault if one of these fuses blows – you will need a continuity tester – a tool that helps detect problems in electrical circuits and components.

3. **MCB (miniature circuit breakers).** The vast majority of homes – and all new installations – will have a consumer unit fitted with MCB fuses. These are trip switches that break the circuit in the event of a problem. They don't need to be replaced, simply reset. If you don't have this type of fuse box, give serious thought to having your fuse box upgraded as this is by far the safest option.

Whatever type of fuse box you're using, the problem of a blown fuse is likely to come down to the same issues – an overloaded circuit or a faulty appliance.

● Switch off the mains power, replace any blown fuses and remove all the appliances.

● Then reinstall them one by one until the fuse blows again.

● Once you've identified your faulty appliance, take it to be repaired professionally.

IF A LIGHT DOESN'T WORK

Another option for system failure is that a bulb has blown, tripping the MCB or blowing the circuit fuse.

● Check all the bulbs in the house – if the bulbs are of the traditional filament variety, you'll be able to tell if one has blown by giving it a gentle shake – the blown filament wire will rattle.

● Replace the bulb and reset the system. If the light is part of a lamp plugged in to the main circuit via a socket, check the fuse in the plug as well as the bulb.

Pocket tip 🔨
Use a soft, dry cloth or tea towel to remove a bulb that's just blown.

IF A CIRCUIT-BREAKER KEEPS TRIPPING OUT

When an MCB continually trips out, this points to one of two possibilities:

- There is a specific problem with one appliance.

- There is a more fundamental problem with the wiring of the circuit.

To test if the problem relates to an appliance, follow the systematic check outlined above. Otherwise you may need to call a qualified electrician to check whether there's a harder-to-find issue.

Rule of thumb ✔

If your electrical system uses a modern consumer unit, it may also contain an RCD (residual current device), an additional safety feature that detects faults in the current. If this device has tripped, the entire circuit will shut down until it is reset.

❯❮ DECORATING ❯❮

WHAT TO DO . . .

IF A HOLE IN A WALL OR CEILING NEEDS FILLING

Assuming we're dealing with a patch, not a major plaster repair (which is a more major job, explained in Chapter 2, p. 69), your options depend largely on the type of plaster you're mending. The two main types are:

- modern plasterboard
- traditional lath and plaster.

Fixing a hole in plasterboard

If the hole is just a couple of centimetres in diameter, you can repair it by using ready-mixed filler or a piece of plaster board joining tape. A larger hole can be fixed by attaching a piece of hardwood that is wider than the hole to the inside of the hole.

- Drill a hole through the hardboard and attach some string to it.
- Fix the hardboard to the hole using wood glue or PVA and hold it fast by pulling the string.
- Once it has set, repair the remainder of the hole with filler as above.
- For a very large hole, cut the damaged board into a regular shape that exposes the batons of the wall.
- Then fix a new piece of plasterboard to the exposed batons using nails or screws.
- Use plasterboard joint tape to mask the join.
- Paint or skim-coat the wall to finish the repair in all cases.

Fixing a hole in lath and plaster

Tap around the damaged plaster with your knuckles to check the state of the surrounding area. If the job is too big for filler, follow the instructions for a major plaster repair outlined in Chapter 2 (see p. 69). Otherwise, make sure you have cleaned the area that you are repairing and build up the layers of filler carefully, no more than one centimetre at a time, allowing each layer to set.

IF YOU BREAK A TILE

Replacing a single broken tile is a tough job and you'll need to take great care to avoid damaging the surrounding tiles.

- First, cut out all the grout around the damaged tile using a grout removing rake. If you don't do this, you will soon have two damaged tiles.

- Once the grout is removed, put a cross of masking tape on the tile to keep the bits of broken tile together.

- Drill a hole in the centre of the tile to the tile's depth and then very carefully begin to break the tile with a hammer and cold chisel, starting at this central hole and working outwards. Wear safety glasses while you work.

Make sure you chisel out the tile and adhesive backing properly to give you a good, even base for the replacement tile.

Pocket tip ↖

When tiling a room, keep back a pack of each variety of tiles you are using in case you ever need a replacement — it'll save you searching round for an exact match in the future.

⚞ OUTDOORS ⚟

WHAT TO DO . . .

IF YOU HAVE MOLEHILLS ON YOUR LAWN

Moles are a nightmare for the gardener. Moles are most prevalent in the spring and autumn and can dig tunnels at a rate of four metres an hour, which means they can lay the average-sized garden to waste in about a day. Most gardeners have their own methods for discouraging moles – ranging from sinking milk bottles into a mole run (the sound of air passing over the mouth of the bottle disturbs the moles) to crumbling dried eucalyptus leaves into the run. In truth, most of these homespun remedies will only succeed in irritating the moles and ensuring they divert their runs, causing even more widespread damage to the garden.

Pocket tip ⚒

If you can't beat the moles, you can at least strive to limit the damage to roots by lining planting holes with fine gauge wire mesh.

The most effective ways to get rid of moles are to trap them or fumigate the runs. Traps and fumigants are available from some DIY stores – follow the instructions carefully, as these products can be dangerous to you and harmful to other pets.

Pocket tip ⚒

One viable alternative to fumigation is to use ant killer powder. This won't kill the moles, but it will make them choose an alternative route.

IF YOU HAVE AN INSECT INFESTATION

Dealing with an infestation of insects rather depends on the type of insect you're blighted with.

Bees

If bees decide to nest in your garden you should really leave them alone, but the exact advice depends on the type of bee you've discovered. Contact your local council environmental health team for advice, but never try to remove the nest yourself.

Wasps

Wasps are a different issue – there's a lot more sympathy for the idea of killing wasps' nests, although again you need specialist help – environmental health should be the first port of call again as they can also provide the cheapest solution.

Ants

For an infestation of ants there are plenty of poisons, powders and other products for self-application, with a variety of results. To stop ants getting into the house, place a ring of ant powder around the perimeter of the house and ensure that holes in brickwork and woodwork are filled.

Flies etc

A lot of insects are attracted by rotting wood, stagnant water or rotten food waste. Minimising these attractions in your garden will reduce the risk of infestation.

IF WATER GATHERS ON A PATH OR PATIO

If 'pooling' of water becomes a problem it is most likely because the path or paving is not level or because it has inadequate drainage. In both cases, your best bet will be to lift the problem slabs and re-skim the concrete layer beneath the slab. Make sure the surface is even.

If you're laying onto a completely flat surface, lay the slab with a 10mm drop from one side of the path to the other. This will allow rainwater to drain away safely to the earth.

IF A GUTTER LEAKS

A gutter will leak if there's a build-up of leaves or other blockages that are preventing rainwater from getting down the drainpipe.

- First, clear the blockage – try a powerful jet of water sprayed up the drain from ground level or clearing from above with drain rods.

- Then create a wire mesh cap for the down pipe and any areas likely to be affected by a build-up of leaves.

Another potential problem comes from brackets slipping away from the soffit – the fascia running beneath the eaves of the house. Check all the brackets and add more if necessary. Slipped brackets can cause the gutter to bow, which will lead to pooling and leaks.

Finally, check all joints between sections of gutter. This is another likely source of leaks, especially if you've recently had a spell of heavy rain or wind. Tap disjointed gutters back together with a rubber mallet.

Pocket tip ↖

You can buy excellent gutter repair mastic that can even be applied in the rain.

IF YOU HAVE A BROKEN ROOF TILE

Replacing broken tiles involves ladder work and is therefore fraught with potential dangers. Never stand on a tiled or slate roof, even if you're using crawling boards.

- A broken tile can be removed by lifting the tiles around the affected one – the tiles immediately above and to the side must be raised (but not removed) to access the damaged one.

- If the tile is nailed in place, use a tool known as a slate ripper to remove the nail and then nail the new tile back in place with a rustproof tiling nail.

Pocket tip ↖

If you cannot get a suitable tile to replace the broken one, slide a sheet of lead under the broken tile and the two either side.

⟩━⟨ GENERAL ⟩━⟨

WHAT TO DO . . .

IF YOU HAVE A DRAUGHTY WINDOW, DOOR, FLOOR OR FIREPLACE

Draughts are problematic if they are wasting precious and expensive energy, but the free movement of air is essential in certain areas of the home.

Rule of thumb ✎

As a general rule, you should avoid draught-proofing rooms where good ventilation is a health and safety issue — mainly kitchens, bathrooms and rooms with fuel-burning heaters. Never block a ventilator or extractor and don't completely block up a disused fireplace — leave space for a ventilation grille.

Apart from the above, draught-proofing makes good economic sense. A range of products are available to seal draughts around doors, windows and in problem areas such as letterboxes. Check that the product you select meets the British Standard 7386.

Pocket tip ✎

Draughty floorboards can be sealed with candle wax or with some PVA adhesive.

Other ways to cut draughts and lower your fuel bills:

● Hang a thick blanket or throw over your front and back doors.

- Use an old-fashioned material draught excluder under doors – a child's cuddly toy snake is always pretty effective.

- If you can't afford double glazing or secondary glazing, fix a sheet of polythene over any windows that aren't regularly opened.

- Buy thicker curtains.

Pocket tip ✎

One of the main causes of condensation in the bathroom comes from running hot, steaming water directly into an empty bath. If you run a covering of cold water first, then add the hot to suit, you'll reduce the amount of condensation at a stroke.

IF YOU HAVE MOULD IN YOUR BATHROOM OR KITCHEN

Mould is a side effect of moisture build-up, which may be a necessary evil in areas such as bathrooms and kitchens that require good ventilation (see above). The first step in dealing with mould is to eliminate existing build-up.

- Use a good-quality mould spray and wipe down all affected surfaces.

- Then remove the moisture from the room – you could hire a dehumidifier or, if it's a persistent problem, consider fitting an extractor fan or cooker hood (see Chapter 3: *Installing Household Appliances* for installation advice for such products).

Pocket tip ↖

If you've cut moisture build-up but you're still getting unnaturally high levels of damp, condensation or mould in your home, check that you don't have a leaking pipe or a failed damp-proof course.

There are plenty of simple steps to reduce moisture in kitchens and bathrooms:

- Keep lids on pans.

- Don't dry clothes in these areas.

- Open windows while cooking or washing.

- Keep constant background heat in these areas.

To minimise future mould build-up, repaint the kitchen or bathroom using a mould resistant or fungicidal paint that is suitable for high-moisture areas.

Pocket tip ↖

To brush up on your DIY skills, or to learn something new, check out free courses and taster sessions at your local DIY warehouse. Many offer basic training in tiling, plumbing or power tool safety, among others.

2

PROJECTS

In this chapter we'll take a step-by-step look at some complete DIY projects inside and outside the house. Each project will mention tools as necessary – for a full list of the tools required for a range of jobs and a brief explanation of their function, see Chapter 4: *Know Your Trades*.

✻ DECORATING ✻

PAINTING

Preparation

If you ask any professional decorator about preparation they will tell you that it is not only very important, but that it takes anything up to about 85% of the decorator's time. So if your idea of preparing an area for painting is to give it a quick flick round with the duster, think again.

DIY Golden Rule No. 2 ✻

Treat decorating as you would a surgical operation – the cleaner you are, the more effective the results will be. Remember: the finish is only as good as the preparation.

Preparation basics

1. Clear the room that you're about to paint. If you have some large items of furniture that will remain, place them in the centre of the room and cover with dust sheets.

2. Remove flaking or damaged paintwork with a paint stripper or heat torch (remember to ventilate the area well and wear a dust mask to avoid inhaling any dangerous fumes).

3. Sand down woodwork and use knotting fluid to seal knots in wood.

4. Use a vacuum cleaner to clear the entire area.

5. Wash all surfaces with a water and sugar soap solution to prepare it and to collect any residual dust.

6. Turn off electricity, then unscrew ceiling roses and power socket fascias. Cover them with plastic food bags to protect them.

7. Protect window glass and any surfaces that are not to be painted with two-inch thick strips of masking tape.

8. Seal any cracked joints between the ceiling and the wall with a flexible, paintable sealant from a tube. It is worth buying a sealant gun because the cartridges are much cheaper than the kinds that have built-in dispensers. Use a wet finger to get a smooth joint.

Preparation is about more than just a tidy room; you need to prepare your materials too. That means choosing the right brush for the job – the biggest one you can comfortably hold. Choose a good-quality brush, otherwise you'll be picking bristles out of the paint all day. The same is true if you're using a roller – don't scrimp on materials if you want good results.

Pocket tip ↖

Use masking tape to collect any dust and loose fibres on a roller before you use it — it'll save you sticking this rubbish to your wall.

Finally, make sure your paint is up to scratch. Mix it thoroughly and don't use an old can that's been hanging around for years; buy fresh paint to ensure a good colour match with any subsequent pots you buy.

While it's possible to get hold of one-coat paints and undercoat primers, for best results you should apply each coat separately. Prime, then undercoat, then finish with a top coat.

Pocket tip ↖

If you are likely to be painting in a rough or dusty environment, pour paint into a roller tray or paint kettle to avoid dipping a dusty or gritty brush into a fresh pot.

Wood, metal and brickwork

If you are painting on a specific surface such as metal or masonry, use a specialist primer for the best results. For more information on the types of paint available and the different uses of paint, see pp. 144–5.

Rule of thumb ↙

The more coats you use, the better the finish.

Smoothing walls – filling holes

In addition to sealing holes between wall and ceiling (see above), fill small holes and blemishes on the walls with ready-mix filler. Leave the filler repair proud of the wall and then sand down with a fine grade sandpaper when it is dry to create a smooth finish.

The natural order

- Paint the ceiling first.

- Next, paint the walls. Take the wall paint over the joint between the wall and ceiling and approximately 5mm onto the ceiling. This will give a straight line to the top of the wall.

- Finally paint the skirting and architrave. Again, take the paint up the wall about 5mm above the skirting to give a smooth straight line.

External painting

Painting the outside of your house is a major job, but in essence it's a very similar process to interior painting, with the notable exception of the fact that weather and heights play a major part in any external work. The fundamental principles of good preparation, clean surfaces and appropriate tools still hold true.

In addition, you should take into account the logistics of such a large-scale job. Divide the job into manageable sections that you can comfortably tackle one session at a time. This will create a more even finish. It's better to split each side of your house into a manageable painting project.

Rule of thumb ✔

Always try to work from the top down.

Be especially careful when working up a ladder for any period of time (for more information on ladder safety, see p. 160).

The paint you use will depend on the finish you want, but you should definitely use exterior-grade masonry paint for the walls, along with appropriate weather-shielding paints for windows, fascia panels and doors.

Painting problems

If something's gone wrong with the finish of your paint job, it's usually pretty easy to trace the source of the issue. Here are some of the more common issues:

- **Flaking or blistering.** This is caused by a lack of preparation. Paint blisters when there's moisture beneath it from plaster that's not dried properly or wood that is damp. Flaking occurs when the paint doesn't adhere to the base – perhaps because of another type of paint beneath. The only remedy is to remove your new coat of paint and start again with a flawless base.

- **Running.** When the paint runs this is a sign that you've used too much paint by overloading your roller. Wait until the paint has dried, then scrape off the worst of it and repaint.

- **Differences in colour.** This may be down to a lack of preparation of the base again. If there are any traces of different colours behind the coat you've applied, or any grease spots on the wall, these will show through. Let the affected areas dry then rub them down and put on a decent layer of undercoat. Repainting after this should produce a more even effect.

- **Lumps and bumps.** Guess what? That's right, you've failed to prepare again. Only this time the culprit is probably a hair-covered brush or dusty roller or it's a result of the dust you've collected from sanding the wall and then failed to vacuum up afterwards. Rub the area down again and repaint.

WALL TILING

Preparation

Before you start tiling you need to know that the existing wall covering will support the tiles.

- Wallpaper must be removed and loose paint must be stripped.

- Smooth the surface before you start, using a one-coat plaster skim.

- If you're tiling onto a plaster skim coat or onto fresh plaster, you must ensure this surface is properly dried out before you start tiling.

Pocket tip ↖

Prime plaster walls with some diluted PVA solution to reduce their absorbency – this will stop your tile solvent from drying out too quickly.

Choosing the tile

- Ceramic wall tiles make an attractive, easy-to-clean wall covering for kitchens, bathrooms and other 'wet' rooms. They are lighter and thinner than floor tiles, which makes them easier to cut and shape, but it also makes them quite fragile and brittle. Make sure you've got more tiles than you need as there will inevitably be some breakages on your first attempt.

- Porcelain tiles are also popular in kitchens and bathrooms, while marble tiles are becoming increasingly common – though they are still an expensive option and require specialist installation.

- Clay tiles are sometimes used as wall tiles, but if they are used in 'wet' areas they should be sealed with a varnish because they are porous and will be prone to damage.

- Other wall tiling alternatives include glass and mosaic tiles, though again these can require a high level of skill to install (see mosaic floor tiles on p. 53).

Rule of thumb ✔

If you're tiling an enclosed area, use smaller tiles as these create an illusion of space.

Removing tiles

If you're planning to retile a room, don't bother removing the old tiles unless they are in a bad way or if they are no longer securely attached. Removing tiles is a dangerous and arduous job that often results in damage to the wall underneath. Instead, tile directly over the top of securely fixed tiles, after filling any holes or gaps that may exist with plaster repair or filler.

Where to start

Tiling feels like a tough job, but in truth it's all down to common sense and a logical approach.

- Set off from a good base line provided by a horizontal batten of wood that's been screwed to the wall in a dead-level position.

- Mark the tile positions for your first row on this batten and then add a second, vertical batten to the end of the row. This allows you to create one row of level tiles that you can then use as your base for the entire room.

- Work in small areas of less than one square metre at a time.

- Apply the adhesive to the wall (not to the tiles) in advance.

- Place the tiles directly on to the surface. Don't slide them into position, otherwise they will cause an uneven spread of adhesive.

- Use tile spacers on every corner to ensure correct distribution.

- Leave the spacers in place until the adhesive has gone off.

Pocket tip ✎

Measure the space and check the coverage of the tiles (details will be on the box) before you start attaching the tiles – if you find you haven't got enough tiles and then cannot find a match, you will waste money and time.

How to finish

Finishing the job can be a challenge after the relatively simple process of laying straight lines of whole tiles. To cut your tiles, hire a specialist cutting machine from a tile supplier. These take a little bit of getting used to, but they are the only way to handle tricky cuts for small filler pieces of tile for edging and filling around pipes and in tight spots. A narrow edging tile may require a bit more adhesive to bond properly to the wall – apply this directly to the tile. Tile-cutting machines also come with an attachment that allows you to cut holes for pipe work.

Pocket tip ⚒

Cutting tiles can be daunting, but some suppliers will do those tricky L-shaped cuts around windows or pipes for you.

Tiling around a basin, toilet or bath

When tiling around odd corners such as the side of a basin or a toilet cistern, use a card template to give yourself an indication of the shape required, then cut the tile with a tile saw.

Remember to use a flexible silicone sealant to fill the gap between the bath's edge and the tiles to ensure no moisture penetrates the back of the tiles. Follow the same procedure down the corner of the wall to seal and to allow for any movement.

Grouting

You can grout tiles from 24 hours after installation. Use a sponge or a rubber spreader to force the grout into the joints between the tiles and then wipe off the excess grout from the tiles with a clean sponge – don't leave it too long or the grout will harden. When the grout is dry, polish the tiles with a clean cloth.

Rule of thumb ⚒

You'll need approximately 1kg of grout for every 3sq m–4sq m of tiles.

Re-grouting a wall

A build-up of mould can cause grout to turn black. Re-grouting between tiles is a lot of effort, involving scraping the grout away with a rake tool. You can often end up damaging the tiles and/or yourself.

You're better off trying to clean the grout with an oxy-bleach or with a steam cleaner. You can buy grout pens that work like correcting pens, effectively repainting the grout.

If you do decide to re-grout, take out around 2mm of grout and replace with quality mould-resistant grout.

Pocket tip 🖎
Make sure you buy quality grout with in-built fungicide and biocide. It costs more than standard grout but it eliminates the need for laborious re-grouting.

WALLPAPERING

Preparation – measuring the room, removing old paper

If you've never hung wallpaper before you can get into a real mess without decent forethought and preparation. Here are some key principles:

- **Choice of paper.** Get the heaviest, strongest paper you can. Vinyl paper is the toughest – it will tolerate manhandling much better than a cheap, thin paper.

- **Choice of pattern.** Novice wallpaper hangers should avoid paper that requires a pattern match between rolls. Instead go for a random pattern or a plain design.

- **Choice of paste.** Again, if you're trying out wallpapering for the first time, it might be better to go for an all-purpose ready-mixed paste. This may be a bit more expensive than other types of paste, but it will help you produce a good finish first time.

● **Buy enough paper.** Measure the room as if it is a box – don't make allowances for doors or windows as you will need extra paper to go round odd shapes. Buy at least one more roll than you need. See the chart below for minimum recommended numbers of rolls (at standard 10m approximate roll lengths).

Total width of area to paper	Wall height (2.3–2.6m)	Wall height (2.6–2.7m)
10 metres	5 rolls (standard length)	6 rolls (standard length)
12 metres	6 rolls	7 rolls
14 metres	7 rolls	8 rolls
16 metres	8 rolls	9 rolls
18 metres	9 rolls	10 rolls
20 metres	10 rolls	11 rolls

When preparing the room for papering, follow the same basic principles of all decorating jobs (as outlined above in the section on painting). Basically, ensure the walls are clean and free of dust, and that whatever surface you're going to be papering is in good condition.

Never paper over old wallpaper; always remove it first, either by hiring a steamer-type paper stripper or by soaking the wallpaper with warm water – adding a dash of washing up liquid helps to break down the old paste. Whether steaming or soaking, remember not to damage the plaster by creating too much moisture – the walls will need to dry out before you paper in any case.

Pocket tip ↖

If you're papering over wall or ceiling plaster that is very dry, apply plenty of 'size' on it first. This is half-diluted wallpaper paste. Allow this to dry completely and it will stop the surface from absorbing too much moisture from the paste.

Clothing and equipment

Before you start, make sure you've got the right kit. You'll need:

● a pasting brush

● a pasting table

● rubber gloves

● a smoothing brush

● a seam roller for the edges

● an apron with a large pouch to carry scissors and a knife.

Making paste

As mentioned above, ready-mixed paste is the simplest option for wallpapering, but it is not the only choice. If you're using vinyl wallpaper in an area with high moisture, you might want to use a specialist fungicidal paste that stops mould. With vinyl you may also need a special adhesive to stick down the overlapping sheets of paper.

Hanging paper

When it comes to hanging paper, there's no substitute for learning by trial and error.

● Start from a good vertical line drawn on the wall just in from one corner of the room.

- Make the line using a plumb line, spirit level and pencil.
- Soak the first sheet of paper in paste.

Rule of thumb ✎

Allow pasted wallpaper to soak for up to five minutes but no longer.

- Once it has been pasted, fold the paper in on itself as this will stop evaporation of the adhesive and will ensure you don't get paste on the front of the paper.
- Leave the paper for up to five minutes before hanging it.
- Paste up a new sheet of paper before hanging the previous one, so that you don't have any unnecessary waiting around.
- Hang the first sheet, making sure you align it with your perfect vertical line.
- Make sure you butt up subsequent sheets to each piece of perfectly plumbed paper and the paper will look okay.
- Pattern matching is especially hard because when paper is pasted it stretches and different sheets will stretch differently according to variations in soaking time.

Pocket tip ✎

If a piece of paper is soaked for too long, you don't need to bin it, just cut it up and use in an unobtrusive place such as over a window. Do the easy bits first, then the fiddly off-cuts.

The fiddly bits

Cornering

One of the first mistakes people make is, when going round their first corner, they push the paper into the corners with their fingers and then carry on. This is wrong, and will ensure that the next wall of paper is hung at an angle.

- Cut the paper just beyond the corner, around half an inch or 10mm.

- Then get another piece of paper and match it into the corner.

Walls are rarely perfectly straight, so if you don't do this you'll end up with a curve and you'll never get the rest of the paper to line up.

Windows

- Paper into the sides of the window reveal first of all, cutting a notch out for the sill.

- Then paper the small sheets above the window, folding these down over the top of the window reveal.

- Finish any gaps at the top left and right corners of the reveal with off-cuts.

Arches

These are very tough for anyone but the seasoned pro – but you can do them if you:

- Paper over the arch opening.

- Carefully cut the paper back around the shape of the arch, leaving just over an inch of paper exposed.

- Notch the exposed paper into little 'tabs' like the ones used on children's cardboard models.

- Stick these tabs into the arch recess and then hang a cut sheet over the tabs to hide them.

Plugs/switches/light fittings
- Hold the paper over the fitting so that you can see where it rests through the paper.

- Cut a small hole with your knife in the middle of the paper and cut back four flaps so that the fitting is almost exposed.

- Turn off the power, remove the fascia plate and trim the paper so that it fits neatly around the cable box underneath the fascia.

- Secure the paper to the wall and reattach so that it just over-laps the cut hole.

Radiators
In an ideal world, you'd drain the radiator and remove it from the room (see p. 13) but more realistically, you'll need to work around radiators by cutting around fixings and smoothing paper down the space behind the radiator using a long-handled paint roller.

Papering ceilings
- Before you tackle the ceiling, make sure the area is clean and minus any previous decoration other than emulsion paint.

- Again, choose a paper that is not too thin and that doesn't have a pattern repeat.

- Start either side of any light fitting in the middle of the ceiling.

- Work in the shortest way across the area (ie, if the room is 10ft × 14ft, cut pieces 10ft rather than 14ft).

The best way to hold the paper is to use a clean (new) paint roller on a pole. You will also need some steps, or ideally a small platform or raised plank, so you can walk the width of the room.

- Draw on the ceiling a pencil or chalk line that is roughly parallel with the wall.

- Then soak the paper as outlined above (or as detailed in the paper manufacturer's instructions).

- Using the extended roller to support the slack, put the paper up roughly so that none is trailing on the floor.

- If you can find someone to assist you at this stage, it helps with the trickiest part of holding one end while attaching the other.

- Using the first piece as a guideline, repeat the operation across the whole room.

Pocket tip 🔧

When you've finished papering a room, keep a record of the number of rolls of paper you used on the wall and/or ceiling and write this on the top of the door (or in a very safe, memorable place). Next time you paper the room you'll have an easy guide for sizing the job.

FLOORING

Tiling floors

At the risk of sounding repetitive, successful flooring depends on the quality of preparation. The floor you're tiling onto is a more important factor than the type of tiles you're going to use. Here are some basics:

- Try not to tile on to tiles, unless they are extremely well secured. In an ideal world, you should break up an old tile floor before you start.

- If you're working on a concrete sub-floor, make sure it is damp-proof. You can use a layer of epoxy screed to ensure any moisture doesn't penetrate.

- Make sure the surface is level before you begin. Again, if you're tiling onto concrete, use a self-levelling compound to even out the sub floor.

- If you're tiling onto wood, lay a bed of pre-treated plywood underneath the tiles as a cushion. If you lay straight onto floorboards, the joints between tiles will crack as the boards shift.

- Make sure all surfaces are clean and dust-free before you start.

- If you're going to be using adhesive to secure the tiles, make sure the room has adequate ventilation.

Planning is essential for success. If you're working in a more or less square room, your first job will be to find a centre point to begin from.

- Draw lines from the midpoint of joining walls; where they intersect is your starting point.

- Lay your tiles (without adhesive) along a central line and work out from here in a cross shape to all four sides of the room. From these trial lines you'll have an idea of the extent of cutting required when you get to the edges and corners.

- If both sides of the room are going to be visible, adjust your central line of tiles so that the cuts are even at all visible edges.

Pocket tip ↖

Use a string line to get one straight run of tiles. Continue to use this line when laying successive rows. Follow the line, not the previous row of tiles.

● When you come to the edges of the room, use a tile cutter or sharp knife to trim the tiles – depending on the covering you've chosen.

● To work around awkward shapes such as architraves and central heating pipes, you need to cut out a cardboard template and use this against the tile you're trimming.

Rule of thumb ↖

Only amateurs tile themselves into a corner. You need to plan your exit – work towards a door you can get out of.

Types of tile

When selecting tiles, follow the general principle that over-ordering is best practice. There will almost certainly be some wastage and you may want to keep a pack back in case of a breakage.

Buy all your tiles at the same time and check the batch numbers to be sure you get a good colour match.

Pocket tip ↖

Mix up the tiles from different packs so that if there is a slight difference in colour or finish it will not be so apparent.

Carpet tiles. These are good for living areas such as lounges, halls and dining rooms. The main practicality of a carpet tile is that they can be lifted and moved around the room to hide wear – or easily replaced in the event of a stain. For this reason you shouldn't stick carpet tiles down with adhesive. Follow the manufacturer's instructions carefully when laying carpet tiles – there is normally a specific order in which the tiles should be laid – this is normally marked on the underside of the tile using arrows.

Cork tiles. Less common and less flexible than carpet tiles, cork tiles are nonetheless useful in a kitchen or bathroom. They provide a comfortable walking surface. Though they are laid in the same way as other tiles, you should take great care when storing cork tiles; don't take them out of the box prior to installation as the corners tend to curl if they are left out for too long.

Ceramic floor tiles. A more hard-wearing tile than the above options, ceramic tiles are harder to lay as they are rigid and more fragile when cutting. With a rigid tile it is also more important to make sure you get a full bed of adhesive – follow the instructions that come with the tiles. You have to make sure there are no cavities or voids because otherwise you'll find that as soon as someone drops a pan or steps on the unsupported tile with a stiletto heel, it will just crack.

Rule of thumb ✏

With ceramic tiles, allow sufficient joint width to deal with any variations in the dimensions and shape of the tiles – at least 3mm, but preferably 5mm will be required.

Other types of flooring

Vinyl sheets. The advantage of vinyl sheets is that there aren't so many joints and gaps to catch leaks and dirt. The disadvantage is that they are large and heavy, making installation a virtual impossibility if you're working alone.

● Store vinyl sheets in the room that they're going to be used in for a couple of days prior to fitting so that they are acclimatised to the room.

● When laying the flooring, use a stiff brush or broom to ensure the vinyl sticks tight to the sub-floor.

Mosaic floors. Mosaic floors are a tough job. They are usually supplied on a sheet, and unless you are good at laying an even bed of adhesive, you can get into a mess laying it as the adhesive can squeeze up between the individual tiles and ruin the whole effect. If you decide to give it a go, a good way to level a mosaic is to use a piece of wood or even a floor tile that's the same size as the mat of mosaic tiles (usually 30cm × 30cm approximately), so as you push down you're spreading the load.

Pocket tip ↖

An even spread is vital with mosaic floors. Another way to get the tiles level is to roll a clean, large paint roller over the top — but be gentle!

Wooden flooring and laminate

These types of flooring have the advantage of being hard-wearing, easy to install and attractive. Laminate flooring is the quicker of the two options — it is laid like a giant jigsaw in a 'click-fix' method that doesn't require adhesive to secure the boards to the floor – hence the term 'floating floor' is often applied to this type of surface.

Laying laminate and wood floors are initially approached in the same way:

- Remove the skirting boards in the room to allow for an expansion gap around the edge of the boards. You can line this gap with strips of cork.

- Ensure you have a decent sub-floor that will give you an even and noise-free structure to lay the boards onto. If you're laying onto a concrete floor, use a damp-proof membrane once the floor has been levelled. Then lay out underlay across the room – this helps with noise reduction. If the surface still isn't perfectly level, lay a thin surface of plywood across the floor, beneath the underlay, to smooth out irregularities.

- After this, begin laying the boards – work from the far side of the room to the door.

Pocket tip ↖

If you're laying new boards over a floor with existing floorboards, lay the new floor at right angles to the original.

One of the main differences between laminate and solid wood floors (apart from price and finish) is that solid wood is nailed together and laminate is glued. When securing solid wood tongue-and-groove boards, you will need to hire a machine known as a 'secret nailer'. This isn't as dramatic as it sounds; it's just a special machine that drives nails diagonally into the tongue of the wood, and is then hidden by the next section as it pushes into place.

Pocket tip ↖

As with vinyl flooring, wood floor needs time to acclimatise in the room. Open the packs of wood and store them in the room for a couple of days prior to installation.

Bare floorboards

If you've got floorboards that are in good condition, with a little preparation you can use them as an attractive and hard-wearing surface.

- First, seal the knots in the wood, plug up any gaps with wood filler and make sure there are no loose nails or screws.

- Then, depending on the state of the boards, you can either sand them manually or, more likely, hire a floor sander to get an even finish.

- Once the floor is sanded to a good, even finish, you can either paint the floor, or if you prefer a natural finish you can varnish or stain the boards. Remember that varnish will improve the durability of the surface.

Pocket tip ↖

When working with any wood stains or varnishes, remember that they can be highly toxic — a dust mask and good ventilation are essential.

⤜ CARPENTRY ⤚

REPLACING A WINDOW OR EXTERNAL DOOR

Updating windows and external doors can have a big positive impact on your property, but any external window or door replacement work must get consent from your local council's building control team. Given the level of work involved in applying for consent and the fees associated with it, this may be a job that's best left to a professional installer, who will handle all the regulations on your behalf.

Rule of thumb ❦

If you undertake any work, structural or electrical, that requires building control consent, but you don't apply for the necessary consent, it will be almost impossible to sell your house in the future.

If you're replacing a front or back door, not replacing the door frame or making any structural alterations, and you have the necessary consent, the process of fitting the door is the same as explained below for internal doors. The main practical difference is that external doors are heavier and therefore require three hinges rather than the usual two.

Pocket tip ❦

Hardwood external doors offer greater security and insulation than UPVC and glass-panelled alternatives.

REPLACING AN INTERNAL DOOR

There are four common varieties of internal door:

- **Panel doors** are the 'traditional' solid-type door, sometimes using hardwood panels, sometimes glass.

- **Moulded doors** resemble panel doors, but they are much lighter – normally constructed from a moulded piece of wood or plastic fibre that is attached to a timber frame.

- **Flush doors** consist of two flat panels nailed to a timber frame with a type of cardboard filler.

- **Fire doors** are used in special locations – such as connecting doors to garages and loft rooms. They are usually constructed in the same way as flush doors, but with much stronger – and more fire-resistant – materials.

Pocket tip ↖

When fitting a new internal door, make sure you know where the lock block is. Internal doors tend to be made out of hardboard with cardboard filler. A timber block is put in the door where the latch, lock or handle is to be fitted.

1. Measure the door frame. Do this top, middle and bottom to check for deviation and, if necessary, pack the door frame with wood or repair it to get a regular shape (see below).

2. Try your door against the frame to make sure it will fit. If you need to take a little off the door, then use a plane and work with the grain of the wood to shave off a few millimetres for a better fit.

Pocket tip ↖

If you're fitting doors before laying carpet or floor covering, take these into account when sizing the door. A gap of 12mm–15mm from the bottom of the door to the floor should allow for any subsequent floor covering.

3. Mark the hinge positions on the door and the frame and chisel out recesses for the hinges.

4. If the old recess on the door frame is too small, chisel out the extra space required. For improved stability don't use old screw holes but make new ones. Consider adding a third hinge if the door is heavy.

5. Screw the hinges to the door.

6. Get someone to help you lift the door into position or use a couple of wedges beneath the door to support it and then attach the hinges to the frame.

7. Use one screw in each hinge, then check that the door opens and closes easily.

8. Then add the remaining screws.

Rule of thumb ✎

If you're using moulded or flush doors which are constructed from simple timber frames, be aware that shaving too much from the timber edges will weaken the structure of the door. Never exceed 10mm at the top and bottom and 5mm on the sides.

REPLACING INTERNAL DOOR FRAMES

You should never try to replace a door frame on a retaining (load-bearing) wall. This will require structural support and should be left to a professional builder. However, replacing a frame on a partition wall is a relatively straightforward job. You can buy ready-sawn kits from DIY stores that are simple to install.

FITTING NEW IRONMONGERY TO A DOOR

Letterbox

To fit a letterbox to a wooden external door:

- First draw a template of the box hole on the outside of the door. Remember to use a spirit level to ensure it is straight and central.

- Then drill pilot holes at each corner of the wood to be removed.

- Cut out the shape for the hole using a jigsaw.

- Then attach the face plate by drilling screw holes from the out-side of the door to the inside and fixing the screws with nuts on the inside of the door.

If your letterbox has an external plate only, fit a draught-excluding flap on the inside of the door to minimise draughts in case the box sticks when it is opened.

Door knocker

As with the letterbox above, measure up carefully to make sure your knocker is positioned correctly, then drill through the door, front to back, to provide holes for the screws that will be secured on the inside of the door with nuts.

Handles (internal doors)

To fit handles to a new door you'll need to measure the length of the square spindle (the long block of metal that runs through the door) to make sure it fits the space correctly. It may need to be trimmed to fit. Measure the job very carefully as you'll need to line up both sides exactly.

● Drill a hole for the spindle to pass through, then mark the fixing holes for the handles.

● Loosely attach one handle and the spindle, then attach the other handle and try the mechanism in place.

● Adjust if necessary and then fix the remaining screws.

Pocket tip ↖

When replacing an existing door handle, try to choose a new unit that will reuse (or at least cover) the screw holes left behind by the old one. This will save you a redecorating job and will keep the door looking better for longer.

⊶ FITTED KITCHENS ⊷

Fitting a kitchen is the ultimate test of DIY skills as it brings together knowledge in plumbing, carpentry, electrics and deco-rating. Electrical and plumbing installations are dealt with in more depth in Chapter 3. Here we take a closer look at the process of creating the framework of a new kitchen.

Pocket tip ↖

A fitted kitchen isn't your only option – freestanding units can create a more flexible work area and have the added advantage of being removable when you want to move house.

It's becoming easier than ever to fit a kitchen to a professional standard – that's because of the advances in kitchen-planning software – computer programs that help you select and arrange the elements of a fitted kitchen until you are completely happy with the results. Most major DIY stores and some furniture retail-ers offer a free kitchen-planning service, which should be your second port of call.

The first port of call is the kitchen itself:

- Make sure you take accurate and detailed measurements of the room, as your plan will only be as good as these measurements.

- Draw a working plan, indicating existing power points, pipe work and the position of doors.

- Also mark where the windows are and which walls are external.

> ### *Rule of thumb* ✒
>
> *Any good kitchen design takes into account the distance between the key 'work triangle' of cooker, fridge and sink. Though these elements of a kitchen should not be adjoining, they should all be easily accessible.*

Even if you're using sophisticated design software, most kitchens follow a reasonably strict pattern of straight lines of units, or possibly L- or U-shaped arrangements. However, if you've got a big space, there's nothing to stop you using a central pedestal unit.

> ### *Pocket tip* 🔨
>
> *If you're taking out an old kitchen, save back a couple of old drawers. They can be useful for holding screws and other fittings.*

When you've got a design that you're happy with and you've bought the units and all associated fittings, you're ready to start the installation. You may obviously have an old kitchen to remove first, and this should be done carefully and methodically to avoid unnecessary damage to the walls. Naturally, if you wish to repaint the area, it makes sense to do this before fitting the new units.

> ### *Pocket tip* 🔨
>
> *While the water waste pipe is exposed, block the end with a kitchen cloth or rag. This will help to prevent debris from any building work from gathering in the waste pipe. It will also prevent drain smells from filling the work area.*

- Begin your installation in a corner.

- Unpack your first cabinet and assemble it on the cardboard packaging to avoid damaging the unit and/or floor.

- Measure the first assembled cabinet and then measure and mark out the wall.

- Using a spirit level, check that the wall and floor are straight and correct, if necessary. You will be able to adjust the feet of the floor cabinet to make it level.

- Once this is done, screw the cabinet to the wall.

- With subsequent cabinets, keep following the line of the first cabinet rather than the line of the wall or floor.

Pocket tip ↖

Don't forget that a kitchen is the perfect place to use salvaged materials — particularly if you want to create a distinctive worktop or utility area.

WORKTOPS

Worktops should be carefully sized, taking into account any deviations in the end wall. This is also the time to cut out any holes for hobs and sinks using a jigsaw. When you have cut the worktop to length, screw it down to the cabinets and seal around the joints using silicone.

Pocket tip ↖

Washing-up liquid makes a good alternative to silicone sprays/gels.

WALLS

When fixing anything to a wall using wall plugs and screws, it is best to use the object to be fixed as a template and drill through the fixing holes to mark the position of the plugs. Use a thinner masonry bit or an old drill bit.

A dustpan held (or envelope taped) against the wall under the drill will collect most of the drillings, making cleaning up easier.

Q How were the kitchen worktops in the *Titanic* fixed down?
A Counter sunk.

➤◄ PUTTING UP SHELVING ➤◄

This is a task that most people feel comfortable tackling, but as with all DIY jobs, poor preparation can lead to a bad job. Here are some guidelines for best results:

- Think carefully about the load on the shelf – this will help you decide on the type of material you use and the number and strength of fixings you'll require.

- Consider the position of the shelf – if it's near a walkway, is it likely to be knocked or damaged?

- Use a spirit level and a ruler to ensure that your shelves are level and, if you're using multiple shelves, that they are evenly spaced.

1. Step one of putting up shelves is to test for cables. Use a cable locator and try to avoid fixing shelves directly above or to either side of power sockets.

2. Use screws and wall plugs that are capable of bearing the load. Masonry screws need to go in to a depth of at least 50mm, wood screws to around 40mm, or more if the load is heavy.

3. If the shelf is shorter than 1m, fix the brackets to the shelf first, then attach the whole unit to the wall. If the shelf is longer or is of a particularly heavy construction, attach the brackets to the wall first, then screw the shelf down on to the brackets.

⊶ HANGING PICTURES ⊶

As with shelving (see above), it is essential to check for cabling before hanging a picture on the wall.

The fixing method you use depends entirely on what you want to hang. As a broad guideline, a single brass hook will hold a standard frame up to 1m × 500mm approximately. Anything bigger or heavier than this will need a double strength hook or ideally more than one hook.

Mirrors and very heavy pictures should be attached to the wall using screws and wall plugs (see p. 132) to give them extra strength. Use D-rings on the back of the mirror and measure/mark out the spacing for the screws on the wall.

'I would be the most content if my children grew up to be the kind of people who think decorating consists mostly of building enough bookshelves.'
Anna Quindlen

✂ PUTTING UP A CURTAIN TRACK OR POLE ✂

Both curtain tracks and poles need to be wider than the window. You'll need about 50mm–100mm overhang each side of the window reveal.

TRACKS

- Hold the track up to the window to make sure you've got the correct size.

- Measure out from the edge of the reveal to find the right point for your end bracket. In addition to being longer, this needs to be about 50mm higher than the window reveal as well.

- Ensure you've got the two end brackets marked evenly on opposite sides of the window.

- Using a spirit level and straight edge, mark out the other wall brackets at regular intervals.

- Check the wall for cabling using a cable locator and then drill holes.

- Then screw the end brackets and other wall brackets into position, making sure you use appropriate wall plugs.

- Clip the curtain track into place using the mounting clips on the wall brackets.

- Place the end stops on the track once it is securely fixed to the brackets.

POLES

- Carefully mark out the positions for the end brackets as above and then drill holes for the brackets as required.

- To give extra strength and support to the curtain pole, fit an extra pole support bracket at the centre of the pole.

- Again, measure carefully before drilling to ensure this fixing is at the same level. Use a spirit level to check rather than relying on the level of the plaster.

> 'If bad decorating was a hanging offense, there'd be bodies hanging from every tree!'
> *Sylvester Stalone*

✂ PATCHING PLASTERWORK ✂

If plaster work has blown – ie, it has ceased to be attached to the sub-structure of the wall – it will need to be replaced. Depending on the size and location of this plaster repair, it may turn into a serious job that requires the services of a professional plasterer.

Rule of thumb ✔

A good way to tell where you will end up with a plaster repair is to tap the wall. If the plaster sounds hollow, it will come off eventually, so you may as well take it off now while it isn't holding up your expensive mirror or family portrait.

Don't try to plaster a large area yourself – anything up to 1sq m should be possible to manage. You can buy ready-mix plaster that is perfect for small repair jobs of around 3mm depth.

● Apply the plaster with a trowel, aiming for as smooth a finish as possible.

● Build up coats and then level off with a good strong stick that has a straight edge on it.

● As the plaster begins to dry, buff it up with the flat of a trowel.

If the repair job is bigger it can be easier to dry-line a wall with plasterboard, large flat sheets of prepared plaster that can be decorated as soon as they are secured.

The two most common methods for securing plaster board are:

● 'Dot and dab' – using lumps of adhesive around the size of a fist at regular intervals to stick the sheets of board to a masonry wall. Hold the board up against the adhesive and place a wooden brace against it to hold it steady for 20 minutes to an hour.

● Screwing the boards straight into stud walls. When screwing into the studs of a partition wall, eight screws top to bottom should fix the plasterboard securely.

If you're working with an uneven wall, combine the above methods by attaching battens to a masonry wall and then screwing your plasterboard sheets into the battens.

Use joint tape to seal the joins between plaster boards, then fill over the tape before putting a thin plaster skim coat over the whole area to finish off.

Why fighting in a DIY store might be a bad idea...
You'd get plastered! or...
You might get a good flooring!

⇥ FIREPLACES ⇤

If you have a disused fireplace that you want to turn into an attractive feature – perhaps surrounding an electric fire or simply as a period feature in the room – you can quickly and easily create a new focal point. Assuming you're starting from a simple opening in the wall, here's a three-step plan to create a fireplace:

1. **Choose a hearth.** This is normally tiled, but you could use a piece of marble or even a wooden hearth, assuming it is just for decorative purposes. The hearth sits centrally in front of the opening.

2. **Fit a back panel.** This is placed onto the hearth and around the opening. It may have to be cut to size. Many types and styles of back panel are available. This panel is normally constructed of a light plastic material that can be securely fixed to the chimney breast with adhesive. Alternatively, it can be fixed to the back of the mantelpiece.

3. **Fit a timber mantelpiece around the back panel.** The mantelpiece should be put into place; mark guidelines to ensure you have it in the correct central location and then fix it into place with screws through fixings known as keyhole plates.

You can, of course, follow the same three-step procedure to re-open a fireplace, but remember to use fire-resistant materials at all stages.

⚒ ARCHITRAVES, PICTURE RAILS, DADO RAILS AND SKIRTING ⚒

These elements add an attractive finish to a room. They require a bit of planning and some specialist tools, but the finished effect is worth the effort.

DADO RAILS/PICTURE RAILS

Like all the other wall fixings described in this section, dado rails have a practical function – they are traditionally intended as protection against chair backs. This gives you some clue as to their correct location, around a metre from the floor. Use a spirit level to help you draw a guideline around the room.

Pocket tip ⚒

If you need to take an old picture rail off the wall, remember that it may well be attached with adhesive and nails/screws. After removing any fixings that you can get to from the front, you should gently lever yourself a gap behind the rail, using a claw hammer or chisel, and then slice down between rail and wall along the length of the rail with a hacksaw blade.

Picture rails are usually attached 300mm–500mm down from the ceiling. Make sure you line up the dado and the picture rail – this will help offset any discrepancy in the distance from floor to ceiling.

● To cut these rails around corners you will need to use a mitre block and saw to achieve perfect 45-degree angles.

- Rails can be attached to the walls using a combination of adhesives and a few fixing screws to hold the rail firm.

- Fill the screw holes and then sand and touch up with paint.

Pocket tip ↖

*When you're fitting dado rails it's easier to sand and paint the rail **prior** to fitting. If the paintwork is damaged during installation, you can simply do a touch-up job.*

SKIRTING BOARD

Skirting works in a similar way to the other fixings outlined above, with the exception that it gets more wear and therefore needs to be fixed more securely to the wall.

- Use mitre adhesive – a particularly strong glue that holds delicate joints firm – to connect the mitred edges around corners. This will give extra strength to the skirting.

Pocket tip ↖

Treat the unpainted flat side of a skirting board before attaching it to a wall. This will help prevent rot.

ARCHITRAVES

An architrave finishes off a door frame and once again provides an extra degree of security for the paintwork from knocks and bashes. Many architraves come as ready-made kits to fit a standard door size.

If you are making the architrave from scratch:

● Follow the guidelines above to create mitred joints, then nail the top piece of the architrave to the top of the door frame, making sure you line it up carefully to get it central on the frame.

● Then add the two vertical pieces of architrave and nail these to the door frame and to the top piece of architrave with an angled nail that cuts through both parts of the mitred joint.

Q How many DIY buffs does it take to screw in a light bulb?
A Only one, but it takes him two weekends and three trips to the hardware store.

✖ ELECTRICAL ✖

GENERAL

Electricity is dangerous and you really need to know what you're doing before tackling any job. Do some detective work before beginning any other work – find out where your main incoming supply switch is and what type of fuses are used in your consumer unit. If you're using old-style cylinder fuses, make sure you've got some spares handy.

The regulations relating to electrical work in the home are explained in detail below, but as a very general guide:

- Work that involves extending circuits in the kitchen, bathroom and outdoors is likely to need a qualified electrician.

- Replacing damaged sockets, light fittings and cable on a like-for-like basis is okay for you to tackle unaided.

UNDERSTANDING PART P BUILDING REGULATIONS

From 1 January 2005 onwards, the Government tightened regulations governing electrical work in the home, making it very hard for the DIY enthusiast to carry out much more than basic repairs and replacements. The new regulations make life safer . . . but also more complicated.

In brief, most work must be carried out by a government-approved electrical installer, who will ensure compliance with building control regulations on your behalf and who will give you a certificate of compliance on completion. You can still carry out work yourself, but you must then take on the responsibility for informing the building control department at your local council before you start and you must have them sign off the work at the end. This process will involve a fee and if they're not satisfied they may end up getting you to use a qualified electrician after all.

The most stringent regulations apply in areas prone to electric shock risks – bathrooms, kitchens and gardens/outbuildings. To give you some guidelines on the scope of works covered by the regulations, there is a table below. The areas highlighted in bold are okay to be carried out anywhere in the home without notifying building control. As you can see, there aren't many of them.

Rule of thumb ✔

Even if you're confident that your planned electrical work is not covered by Part P, check with the building control team before you start. Ignorance is no defence, and if you make a mistake it could cost you a lot of hassle – as well as being potentially life-threatening.

Nature of work	Kitchen, bathroom, garden	Other areas
Complete rewiring	N	N
Change of fuse box or consumer unit	N	N
New socket in an existing circuit	N	Y
New light switch in an existing circuit	N	Y
Replacing damaged socket, ceiling rose, etc.	Y	Y
Replacing damaged cable on single circuit (like-for-like)	Y	Y
Connecting a cooker to an existing circuit	Y	Y
Fitting low-voltage lighting	N	N
Fitting a storage heater	N	N
Fitting a new power supply to an outbuilding	N	N
Adding socket or light to an existing outbuilding circuit	Y	–
Fitting a solar power supply	N	N
Fitting electric floor heating	N	N
Fitting a generator	N	N
Fitting an immersion heater	Y	Y
Fitting low-voltage wiring for telephone or related equipment	N	Y
Fitting a socket outdoors	N	N
Fitting an electric shower with different kW rating	N	–
Fitting a garden pond pump to the fixed electrics	N	–
Installing an electric sauna	N	–

N = Building control notification required if you undertake the work yourself or use a qualified electrician.
Y = You can undertake the work yourself

WIRING A PLUG

> ### Rule of thumb ✨
>
> *When wiring a plug, remember red or brown wire is live, blue or black is neutral and green/yellow or bare is earth.*

- Unscrew the plug.

- Strip the insulation from the flex to expose the core wires.

- Lay the wires over the open plug and trim the wires to the right length.

- Remove the insulation from the wires, loosen the screws of the pillar terminal and insert the wires into the correct terminal (see diagram).

- Re-tighten the screws to clamp the wires in the terminals and make sure the wires are tight and secure.

- Then clamp the flex into the cord grip at the entrance to the plug.

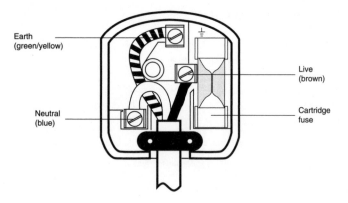

Earth
(green/yellow)

Live
(brown)

Neutral
(blue)

Cartridge
fuse

REPLACING A FLEX

This may be necessary if you have damaged a flex or if you wish to extend one. The biggest challenge here is to work out how the flex is connected to the appliance. You may well need specialist tools to open the appliance – and remember that opening an appliance often invalidates any manufacturer's warranty on it.

Pocket tip ↖

If you do manage to get the appliance open, keep a piece of parcel tape handy to place all the small fixing screws on. It will hold them secure until you have a need for them later.

Remember that any replacement flex you buy must be the right rating – these range from 0.5mm flex for lamps up to 1.5mm for larger appliances. Check with the electrical retailer for the exact rating required for specific appliances.

- When you have exposed all the old cable, prepare your new flex in the same way as outlined above for plugs and examine how the appliance is connected to the original flex in the terminal block.

- Copy this connection with your new flex, ensuring all connections are tight and secure.

- Replace the casing and all the screws and check that the appliance is working again.

REPLACING A POWER SOCKET

If you break a socket fascia or simply want to upgrade to a newer design:

- Switch off the power at the mains and unscrew the fascia.

- Keep hold of the fixing screws just in case the ones you've been given with the new fascia don't fit the mounting box.

- Unscrew the cables from the terminal and remove the old fascia plate, noting the position of the cables in the terminal.

- Copy this order when adding your new fascia.

Pocket tip ↖

A good way to add an extra socket is to buy a plug-in expander, which gives you up to four extra sockets from one existing by just plugging in.

IDENTIFYING A FAULTY CIRCUIT

If an MCB in your consumer unit keeps tripping out – or a fuse keeps blowing in your old-style fuse box – there is a fault on the circuit and the source of this is likely to be one of two areas.

1. **Overloading on the circuit.** This is an easy problem to remedy. Check all the appliances you're using on a circuit to see which power-hungry appliances are causing the overloading, then switch appliances around to give a more even spread across the whole wiring circuit.

2. **Short circuit.** This is a trickier one. Check all the appliances, sockets and other outlets for obvious signs of damage – scorch marks and cracks are tell-tale signs. Then replace the damaged appliance or socket. If this doesn't work or there's no apparent damage on the circuit, you'll need to call a suitably qualified electrician to investigate the problem further.

WHEN DOES A HOUSE NEED REWIRING?

> *Rule of thumb* ✔
> *Household wiring should be checked every 10 years and replaced at least every 20 years.*

It's hard to give a specific judgement on when a house should be rewired, but there are certainly some danger signs to look out for:

- If there's rubber or cloth wiring in the loft, you definitely need to rewire. Have it inspected by a competent electrician as soon as possible.

- If the fuse box uses old wired or cartridge fuses, have this replaced by a modern consumer unit with MCBs and an RCD.

- If you find any exposed wire – ie wire without an insulating sheath – this needs to be covered, but it's also an indication that your system is out of date. If you find any bare earth wire within a terminal, sheath it with green and yellow PVC insulation.

- Check sockets and around the pins of plugs for scorch marks and always be aware of burning aromas around sockets. These are tell-tale signs that there are poor connections.

- Rubber wiring anywhere in the house – particularly from the consumer unit – is a danger. Rubber has a short lifespan as an insulating material, meaning that any of these wires are a potential fire hazard.

- If you have any old two-pin plug sockets in your house, your wiring system is likely to be at least 40 years old.

Pocket tip 🔨

Most electricity suppliers will check your wiring for free — however, they will almost certainly tell you it needs renewing!

LIGHTING

Types of light bulb

Tungsten filament bulb

For many years these have been regarded as 'standard' bulbs, but because they use considerably more energy than other types of bulb, as of 2009 they are being phased out, although they are and will remain widely available for a while at least.

Basic lights come in two types of fitting — screw or bayonet — and in a range of wattages (the measure of electricity a bulb consumes), commonly ranging between 40W, 60W and 100W, depending on requirements.

These types of bulb are used as the main lighting in a room — they give off a yellowish glow.

Halogen

Halogen bulbs are smaller and more energy efficient than tungsten bulbs. The light they produce is whiter and harsher. They are often used in strips of four or five miniature bulbs within a light fitting to create strong directional lighting in a kitchen or hall.

Compact fluorescent

The most common type of compact fluorescent bulb is the 'energy-saving' bulb. These curved fluorescent tubes have come a long way from the harsh strip lights beloved of schools, hospitals and 1970s kitchens. Their wattage ratings range from 9W–23W, as they use a fraction of the energy of tungsten lights to produce similar effects.

At the bottom end of the compact fluorescent market – the kind of bulbs you are given free by your electricity company – the bulbs are quite inflexible. They cannot be used with dimmer switches and security lighting as there is an electronic control circuit inside the bulb which is sensitive to being dimmed, causing the dimmer switch to fail and potentially catch fire. But top-end compact fluorescents are compatible with both dimmers and other forms of timer-controlled lighting – just not with your wallet!

Types of lighting

The type of lighting you choose will be determined by the room's function. The amount of light emitted by a bulb is measured in **lumens**.

As a rough guide, a 60W tungsten bulb gives off about 600 lumens, or around 10 lumens per watt. Other types of lighting – especially fluorescent bulbs – give off considerably more light. Some are as bright as 40 lumens to 50 lumens per watt.

- The brightest rooms are those which are traditionally associated with fluorescent bulbs – kitchens, utility rooms and workshops.

- Living rooms, bathrooms and halls need about half the amount of light that a kitchen needs and bedrooms need about a quarter of that amount.

- Bedrooms and living rooms make up their extra lighting with lamps for specific purposes, such as a halogen reading light next to a chair or bed.

Rule of thumb ✎

Spotlights and halogen lights shouldn't be used as the main focal lighting in a room unless there is a lot of ancillary lighting in the form of standard lamps and table lamps.

Replacing a light switch

One-way switch

Replacing a one-way light switch is a fairly simple process, akin to replacing a power socket. The same basic principles apply.

- First, switch off the power supply and, for safety's sake, remove the MCB or fuse for the lighting circuit from the consumer unit.

- Next, remove the front plate by undoing the two fixing screws. As you remove the plate, note how the cable is wired into the terminal.

- Release the wires and fix into your new switch in the same way.

- If any of the cables are bare, sheath them in correctly coloured PVC before replacing them.

Two-way switch

A like-for-like replacement of a two-way switch uses the same process as the above, but with twice as much cable. However, you should be extra cautious when replacing a two-way switch. If your lighting circuit has been properly wired, both connections within the mounting box will be part of the same circuit. But that doesn't necessarily follow, and one may well be live. So always shut off the mains power or disconnect all MCBs relating to the lighting circuits of your house to be extra safe.

Dimmer switch

Adding a dimmer switch follows the same simple process outlined above, but remember that you cannot operate compact fluorescent bulbs (such as low-energy bulbs) or a fluorescent tube off a dimmer switch (see above).

Rule of thumb

The normal combination for a light fitting is a metal mounting box and a plastic faceplate. In this combination only the mounting box must be earthed. However, if you change the faceplate for a metal type, you must also earth the faceplate.

Installing a new light

Adding a new light switch

If you wish to add a new light switch or install a light in a kitchen or bathroom, your work will need to comply with Part P building regulations. In short, it may be more cost-effective to use an electrician.

However, you can add extra switches for new lights elsewhere in the house. The following is a brief guide, but you must take great care with any new electrical installations – always double check your work and, if in doubt, use an expert.

Decide where you want to place the new light and drill a hole in the ceiling to mark where the ceiling rose will go. Ideally the rose should be fixed to a joist to give it extra strength.

- Mark out the location of the mounting box on the wall and cut out a recess for the box.

- Cut out a run from the mounting box straight up the room and into the ceiling void above.

- Run a length of cable from the ceiling rose to the mounting box.

- Prepare the cable at the mounting box end and place the wires into the correct part of the terminal block (red to the top and black to the bottom).

- Connect the earth to the mounting box, making sure it is properly covered in green and yellow PVC.

- Make sure the cable running from the switch to the ceiling rose is encased in rigid conduit.

- Then attach the cable to the ceiling rose, taking care to follow the manufacturer's instructions to wire the cables to the correct terminals. If in doubt, switch off the power at the mains and check another ceiling rose to see how the system is connected.

You will then need to extend the lighting circuit from an existing light fitting, or from a junction box.

- First, switch off the power and disconnect lighting circuit MCBs.

- Again, check the wiring carefully to make sure you follow the correct order and then attach cable from your new ceiling rose to the existing rose or junction box.

- Finally, attach the pendant flex to the correct terminals in the ceiling rose.

Pocket tip ↖

If you don't feel confident extending the lighting circuit of your home, you can get standalone 13amp lights which plug in to the main circuit. Check lighting retailers for options.

Loft lights

You can wire a loft light using the same method described above, but remember a pendant light isn't necessarily the best option in a loft space where bright lighting may be preferred. Choose a fluorescent strip light for greater effect.

✖ HOME SECURITY ✖

INSTALLING A SMOKE ALARM, FIRE ALARM OR BURGLAR ALARM

Smoke alarms

It goes without saying that every home needs at least one smoke alarm on each floor. The hall and upstairs landings are the most common locations, but you might also want to put extra alarms in children's bedrooms and anywhere that you run appliances at night – a laundry room, for example. Don't install an alarm in a kitchen or directly above a radiator or other heat source.

Smoke alarms are easy to install and usually come with all the fittings required.

- Most alarms have a back plate that needs to be screwed to the ceiling, ideally into a joist, using two screws and wall plugs.

- Once you've secured this back plate, install batteries into the alarm itself, attach it to the back plate (usually it's a twist-and-click locking mechanism) and test it.

You should continue to test the alarm on a regular basis to ensure the battery is still functioning.

Fire alarms

Domestic fire alarms work in a similar way to smoke alarms, except they are triggered by a rise in temperature rather than by smoke. They are fitted in the same way as smoke alarms, but again location is important – don't site them near heat sources or in hot places such as kitchens and bathrooms.

Burglar alarms

There are two types of burglar alarm: wired and wireless. The wired alarm is a major job to fit as it needs cabling from all sensors to the control unit. A wireless unit is the preferred option as it gives the same level of security with minimal cabling.

Both types of alarm use the same combination of detection equipment – sensors which tell if a door or window has been opened (when a contact is broken) and PiR (passive infrared) sensors, which detect movement.

Before you buy a system, work out how many sensors of each type you need and if there's any good reason – such as the presence of pets – why you should avoid a particular type of sensor. The whole kit should be available from any good DIY store and fitting is pretty intuitive.

You will need to find a safe and secure location for your alarm control box. The hall is a popular location – but be sure to place any keypad or control mechanism out of the reach of children.

Pocket tip ↖

Alarm systems can be ignored by neighbours, so if you've got something really valuable to protect, make sure your alarm is of the type that alerts the police when your property is breached.

The all-in-one option

It's possible to buy extremely effective wireless burglar alarms which also have the ability to add modular smoke detector and fire alarm facilities. The great advantage of these in terms of DIY is that no wires are involved, it's very simple and you only need a connection to a phone line and one to a power source. You'll need to change the batteries every two years. But otherwise it's straightforward, hack-proof and tamper-proof.

Pocket tip 🔨

It's important to remember that if you do fit an alarm your-self, it may not be recognised by your home insurers.

FITTING NEW BOLTS AND LOCKS

Window locks and extra door bolts are the simplest and most efficient form of security measure for your home. The best locks available carry the British Standards kite mark and carry the BS code 3621. Place bolts top and bottom of the door and install a mortise lock about a third of the way up the door.

To install a mortise lock into a wooden door:

- Measure the width of the door to make sure you buy the right size of lock body.

- Drill out a mounting for the lock body and then use a chisel to create a recess for the faceplate of the lock.

- Place the lock against the door and mark through the keyhole of the lock to give you an idea of where the keyhole will go.

- Once the mortise is fixed in place, position the keep plate (which is attached to the door frame) so that the deadbolt mounts into it securely.

INSTALLING SECURITY LIGHTING, CCTV

Security lighting and CCTV are both effective burglar deterrents but will require Part P Building Regulations approval from your local building control office because they involve extending the electrical circuit of your house outside. If you want to avoid the extra effort of Part P, you can get low-level lighting that is battery operated or that works using solar power. These will not give the same degree of protection as motion-sensitive lighting, but most burglars will think twice before going into a lit area.

DEFENSIVE PLANTING

There are plenty of other ways to deter burglars from snooping around your property. Most break-ins occur at the back of the property, so focus your defensive measures there.

- Place thorny or sharp-leaved bushes – such as hollies – around windows.

- Use gravel on paths.

- Make sure you don't place items such as wheelie bins in such a way as they can be used as a step up and over your garden wall.

- Don't leave rocks, bricks or other items lying around that the opportunist burglar could use to smash glass.

- Always lock your shed door – even if you don't keep any high-value items in there, a burglar will find plenty of tools and other items to help him gain access to your house.

⊶ INSULATION ⊶

LOFT INSULATION

The main point about loft insulation is this: the more the better. Insulating the loft, lagging pipes and draught-proofing will potentially save you hundreds of pounds a year.

The loft is the main culprit. Hot air rises — and we all know the difference that putting on a hat can make in cold weather. So even if your house already has some loft insulation, it is worth upgrading to improve efficiency.

Rule of thumb 🖌

The recommended thickness of loft insulation is 270mm, although some modern insulation materials are available that provide greater energy efficiency but are not so bulky. Check the packaging for the 'R' rating of the insulation — the higher the rating, the greater the efficiency.

When it comes to laying the insulation, be careful.

- If you're not steady on your feet, or if you have poor lighting in your loft, use a torch (a head torch is great) and take treading boards up with you, otherwise you can risk falling through your ceiling.

- Always wear a dust mask, even if you're using an insulation material that doesn't contain harmful fibres, as your loft will be full of dust, soot and other deposits that you won't want to breathe.

- Wear gloves and a long-sleeved shirt. Don't insulate on a hot day as your loft can get extremely hot and uncomfortable.

Lay the insulation material loosely between the joists and ensure that any electrical cables are clear of the insulation. While you're working in the loft don't forget to lag your water tank and any pipes as well – this is especially important after you've insulated, as it will leave uninsulated pipes in the loft more prone to freezing.

WALL INSULATION

Wall insulation takes two basic forms: dry wall insulation and cavity wall insulation.

If you have a single brick external wall, for example on a small extension or porch, you have a potential source of heat loss. If you don't mind the loss of some internal volume, you can insulate these areas for better efficiency using plasterboard.

- Choose an insulating wall board, which is plasterboard with polyurethane or polystyrene bonded to the back of it.

- Attach this to the brick wall with screws or a non-reactive adhesive. You could use the 'dot and dab' adhesive method (see p. 69).

Cavity wall insulation is a much bigger job. There are two main types of insulation: one is polystyrene bead for houses with a narrow cavity, such as those built between the 1940s and 1960s. The other is blown fibre for bigger cavities. Both types of cavity wall insulation should be installed by a specialist contractor.

PIPE LAGGING

It pays to lag all exposed pipe work around the house – not just the loft pipes mentioned above. If you have an airing cupboard, or any rooms with exposed pipe work, use lengths of foam lagging around the pipes.

Pocket tip ⚒

If you have radiators on an outside wall, buy some heat-reflecting sheets to stick behind the radiator. These bounce the heat back into the room rather than letting it warm the bricks. If you want a cheaper (though slightly less efficient) alternative, use silver foil.

DOUBLE GLAZING

While window replacement is best left to the experts (see p. 56), you can easily fit secondary glazing to windows in your home. These are available as kits and provide you with an extra layer of window that you fit into the reveal of the existing window frame.

- Attach the frame of the second window to the wooden frame.

- Glass panels for this extra window slide into place or are hinged to give access to the main window.

- Finish around the edge of the new window frame with silicone sealant to ensure a draught-proof seal.

Pocket tip ⚒

For more advice on saving energy and reducing consumption in the home, take a look at the website of the Energy Saving Trust: www.energysavingtrust.org.uk

⟞ OUTDOORS ⟞

FENCES

Before you begin a fencing project, ask yourself some questions:

- Do you want the fence to give you total seclusion or just mark a boundary?

- Do you want to be able to remove the fence panels, even temporarily?

These questions will give you some idea of how to move forward and of which option to choose.

First of all, if you're going to erect a fence over 2 metres in height, consult your neighbours about your plans and check with the local council as to whether there are any planning issues with such an imposing structure.

If you're going for a more modest project, then your next thought should be design.

- A picket fence structure can look great, and can be a very rewarding project to build yourself, but it doesn't afford any privacy.

- A higher larch-lap style overlapping panel fence is less appealing but it does screen your garden effectively.

- Ready-assembled fence panels are by far the easiest option, leaving you with the task of fixing posts.

Pocket tip ↖

Remember that even though you're working outdoors, some of the basics of home DIY safety still apply. Before digging any deep postholes you should check for pipes running beneath the ground. Hire a specialist cable locator to make sure you don't damage a key utility pipe.

To fix concrete posts quickly and easily, you'll need to hire some kit – a post-hole borer that looks like a giant corkscrew is a must for getting to the required depth without breaking your back – and a post driver – a long, heavy metal tube with handles that you use to whack the post into the ground.

Rule of thumb ✔

At least a quarter of the fence post must be below ground. A standard 1.8m fence will require a 2.4m post.

Use metal post spikes to secure wooden fence posts. They are strong, easy to use and they lessen the chance of rotting. You can also get spikes that have a bolt which unscrews to allow you to remove the wooden posts from the metal spikes if you ever need to remove a couple of panels.

When you come to measure up for the space between posts, measure each one individually, as dimensions can sometimes vary. Once the posts are secured, nail or screw the fence panels to the wooden posts. Concrete posts have a moulded groove that holds the panels in place.

Pocket tip 🔨

Don't concrete in wooden posts — they will rot off at the top of the concrete in no time.

Cap your wooden fence posts with wooden/plastic or felt ends to keep them watertight, or cut them off at an angle to help rainwater drain away. This will stop rain penetrating the sawn end of the post and rotting the timber.

POINTING

To re-point brickwork:

- Scrape out dried, flaky or failed mortar between bricks to a minimum depth of 10mm. Use a chisel or bolster.

- Once you have cleared out all the loose material and brushed down the brickwork to remove dust, replace the old mortar with a fresh mix.

- Smooth the new mortar into the gap with a trowel.

Pocket tip 🔨

As this will not give an exact match to the mortar used else-where on the wall, it can be useful to re-point complete walls at a time, rather than just patching.

RENDERING

Rendering is a much bigger job than pointing — it's more akin to plastering and for this reason larger rendering jobs are best left to skilled professionals. However, there's nothing to stop you practising your rendering skills on a smaller project – a garden wall for instance or just patching a hole or crack in existing render.

Preparation is a big part of any rendering job, large or small.

- You need to tackle the job in the right atmospheric conditions; don't render when it's very warm, cold or wet outside.

- If you're applying render from scratch, you need to start off from a bell casting, a metal extrusion that holds the bottom of the render in place, and work upwards.

- Work in levels, allowing each to go off before you start on the next.

Rendering normally consists of cement or lime and cement mortar. Although the finish doesn't need to be as smooth as internal plasterwork, it is hard to match the colours of the individual batches of mortar, leaving the finished job with a 'blotchy' appearance which will ultimately need to be painted.

To repair render in a small area:

- Rake out the loose render with a cold chisel and make sure the area is clear and clean.

- If the area is very small, you can use an exterior-grade filler to mask the damage; if the coverage is a bit wider, you'll need to use an undercoat (you can buy these ready mixed), which will need to be smoothed into the hole about 5mm below the level of existing render.

- Once this is dry, apply the top coat. Don't worry if it is slightly proud of the other render as you can level it off with a straight-edged piece of wood.

DECKING

Decking is a useful and less permanent alternative to a patio in the garden. Preparation is easier than for a patio as the deck doesn't require any foundation if laid on dry, flat areas.

- Cut away any lawn below the area to be decked. It's also a good idea to lay weed-proof membrane beneath the sub-frame.

- Secure this with pea gravel.

- Using a piece of wood and a spirit level, ensure that the ground is level.

Rule of thumb ✎

Although a basic deck doesn't require foundations, a raised deck — which is often used as a solution in sloping gardens — is a structure and needs a solid foundation underneath.

- Next you need to build your sub-frame, which consists of a square timber frame strengthened by joists. The joists should be laid at intervals of approximately 400mm.

- Unlike wooden flooring, decking doesn't interlock so you need to create an even spacing between the boards as you lay them to allow for expansion and contraction. Leave a gap of about 15mm–20mm between boards, which you can mark with decking spacers.

- The boards should also have a slight overhang around the edges of the frame.

- To secure the boards you need special stainless steel decking nails – known as brads – or decking screws. Nails can be easily inserted using a hired nail gun, but the advantage of decking screws is they allow you to re-site the boards.

Pocket tip 🔨

Decking tiles are a simpler alternative to boards – they are easier to handle and can be more easily replaced if they get damaged.

PATIOS

- Mark out the area that you're going to pave.

- Cut down through the grass or topsoil to a depth of 150mm–200mm.

- Put a hardcore base layer in the hole and compact it down with a hired whacker.

- Add a thin top layer of sharp sand and level it out. Ideally, you still need 50mm space in the hole plus the depth of the slabs.

- Loosely lay the slabs on top of this base layer to make sure you've got your measurements right and then put a layer of mortar in the hole. Lay the slabs carefully on top, working slowly and carefully.

- Use spacers between slabs to keep an even distance. Remember that a flat surface needs at least a 10mm per metre drop across its width to allow for drainage.

- Don't slide the slabs into place, even if they are very heavy. Sliding them will just make the mortar uneven.

- Use a rubber mallet to tap the slabs into place and fill the gaps between the slabs with a dry mortar mixture of one part cement to three parts sharp sand.

- Brush this into the gaps with a stiff broom.

BRICK WALLS

Walls need foundations and this should be your first step. Dig down 150mm for a 1m wall and fill the foundation with concrete. Let it set before you begin building the wall.

Once you've got your first foundation, you can start laying the wall. A single-brick thickness wall shouldn't be higher than 1 metre – if you need a wall that's higher or one that acts as a retaining wall, you should get expert assistance.

- Mix up some mortar for your wall – usually this is one part cement to six parts sand. Use a suspended board to mix up the mortar and only do small batches at a time.

- Lay a run of mortar on the foundation and put your first brick in place.

- Use a rubber mallet to gently tap the brick into a secure footing and then use your spirit level to check it is flat.

- Spread some mortar on the next brick with a trowel and lay this brick next to the first one. Continue until you have completed the first course of bricks.

- Lay the next course so that their vertical joints are at the midpoint of those in the first course – you will need to halve some bricks using a mallet and bolster. By laying the bricks in this way you will create a 'staggered' effect that gives the wall more strength.

- As you continue to lay the courses, keep checking the levels – both vertical and horizontal – to make sure the brickwork is level.

- Trim off surplus mortar with your trowel, making sure you don't leave any mortar to dry onto and stain the bricks.

- Finally, finish the top of the wall with 'coping' – normally a ridged concrete block designed to stop water penetrating the wall.

BRICK BBQ

A brick BBQ will follow the same basic structure as a brick wall, but you will need to lay some bricks in the sides and rear of the structure at an angle so that they protrude inwards to provide you with brackets for your BBQ grill and ash pan. Remember, you will still need foundations for a BBQ if you want it to be safe and secure.

GREENHOUSES

Like all structures, greenhouses depend on a solid base. Some greenhouse kits come with a steel base that the structure rests on top of, but this is not essential. A concrete foundation *is* vital, however, and should be laid to at least 100mm depth.

- Make sure the concrete base is completely level using a strip of wood and a spirit level.

- Lay a single course of bricks on top of the foundation. The greenhouse structure will be attached to these bricks to give it extra strength and stability.

The greenhouse itself will come as a 'flat pack' unit and must be assembled according to the manufacturer's instructions. It's best to clear a large work area so that you can lay out the structure as you begin to assemble it. As you assemble the various parts of the frame, leave the screws loose until you're happy that the structure is level. Only then should you tighten the screws to the full extent.

Place the glass into the completed structure as the final element of the process. Remember to wear protective gloves and goggles as you install the glass. It is safer to begin with the roof glass and work your way down, but check the manufacturer's installation guide for exact details of how to fit the glass.

SHEDS AND OUTBUILDINGS

Start by laying a concrete foundation for the shed that allows for approximately one inch overhang on all sides. You can place paving slabs or bricks onto this foundation to raise the shed higher and lessen the likelihood of groundwater penetrating the shed and rotting the structure. Using your spirit level, make sure the foundation and any covering are level.

Pocket tip ↖

If the shed is going to take a lot of weight, you need to use a whacker plate to compress the ground underneath it.

- Stand the back end of the shed on the base and prop it up.

- Then lift a side panel up and screw them together at the top, middle and bottom.

- Fix the other side panels and door end in the same way.

- Add the roof support panel and then secure the roof panels.

- Finally, secure the whole structure to the concrete base, making sure that the shed is square on the base.

You'll need to felt the roof of the shed to make it watertight.

- Starting at the bottom edge of the roof, lay the felt in horizontal strips.

- As you work towards the apex of the roof, the felt strips should overlap the lower ones.

- Nail the felt into place with roofing felt tacks and stick the overlapping edges down with felt adhesive to give extra protection against wind damage.

- Finally, fix wooden batons to the roof on a vertical line.

PATHS

To lay a strong, long-lasting concrete path, you'll need to dig a foundation layer of 100mm or so and then put down a layer of coarse building sand. Flatten down and level off the sand and then cover this with pre-cast concrete slabs or mix up some concrete yourself.

If you're using slabs, allow a 10mm gap between them and fill this afterwards with a dry mix of cement and sand brushed well in.

Paths, like patios and other flat concrete structures, should have a gradient of 10mm drop across every metre to allow for rainwater run-off.

Rule of thumb ✎

Concrete paths should never be laid as one continuous strip – you must allow space for expansion of the concrete, otherwise the path will just crack. Place a 40mm–50mm strip of hardboard edging into the wet concrete every 2 metres and these will act as expansion joints.

PONDS

Flexible liner ponds

- Mark out the shape you want the pond to follow, then dig your hole to the necessary depth.

- Before you place the liner in the hole, check for stones, roots and other obstacles that might tear the liner.

- Line the hole with sand.

- Place the liner over the hole and weigh it down around the perimeter with bricks or stones.

- Fill the pond with water and smooth out the liner to create a neat finish.

- Once the pond is full of water, take away the weight supports around the perimeter and trim the liner to fit.

- Leave 200mm overhang, which should then be covered over by your permanent edging.

- Choose bricks or stones for a natural finish.

Fixed liner ponds

Regular-shaped pond liners can be turned on their heads and the shape marked on the ground. Irregular shapes should be marked on a template.

- Measure the pond's depth and dig down.

- Allow a few millimetres extra to accommodate a bed of sand to protect the liner from stones and other ground obstacles.

- Then place the liner into the hole and fill with water.

OTHER GARDEN STRUCTURES

Pergolas

A pergola is normally erected onto a decking base and requires a solid foundation footing – just like heavy fence posts. Consequently, at least one quarter of the vertical posts will need to be below ground level to make the structure secure. Pergolas often come in flat pack kits, ready-sawn and treated, requiring the installer simply to fit the pieces together and secure them with appropriate fixing bolts.

Compost bins

It's possible to make your own compost bin from a wooden frame, but as with all organic material, wood will ultimately rot and you will have to start again from scratch. This is one of those areas where you may be better off buying a plastic bin – they're hardwearing and relatively cheap if bought through a local council-backed scheme.

Pocket tip 🖎

For information on composting – including details of how to build a compost bin, check out the Centre for Alternative Technology website at www.cat.org.uk

Log/coal stores

A fuel store shares many of the principles of the other structures mentioned above. By far the strongest structure would be a three-sided brick arrangement (similar in shape to a brick BBQ) with a concrete base.

- Build the back wall a couple of brick courses higher than the side walls and step the sides up to meet it.

- Then fix a felted wooden roof to this sloping top of the structure.

Rule of thumb 🖌

Concrete structures for anything heavier than pedestrian traffic — ie driveways, hard-standing for cars, summerhouses or other heavy-duty structures — should have a sub-layer of hardcore beneath the foundation. The hardcore should be the same depth as the concrete base — so for a parking space, the concrete floor should be 150mm and the hardcore layer beneath should be 150mm, making a combined depth of 300mm.

'I was in B&Q the other day when this bloke in an orange overall comes up to me and says "Do you want decking?" Well, luckily I managed to get the first punch in!'

⚒ DON'T PUT OFF UNTIL TOMORROW . . . ⚒

When you've completed a hard day's project work, the last thing you want to do is tidy up after yourself. But if you don't pick up the mess and clean your tools, you're creating a whole load of extra work for yourself the following day. Particular areas to watch out for include:

● Stripped wallpaper, plaster and filler left to dry on floors or walls. Almost impossible to shift after a while – work away with the blade of a craft knife or chisel. But take care not to damage the surface.

● Layer of rust on tools left outside. A wipe with an oily rag should restore tools to working quality. Wipe them over as a matter of course at the end of every day.

● Hard paint brushes. Don't leave them to soak in white spirit as this will ultimately damage the bristles. Brush out stiff pieces of paint with a wire brush.

3

INSTALLING
HOUSEHOLD
APPLIANCES

This chapter deals with some of the most common installations you might consider tackling. Some of the projects below will require building regulations approval, and this is indicated where necessary. You're not advised to take on those projects alone unless you are extremely confident and experienced.

❯❮ KITCHEN/UTILITY ROOM ❯❮

INSTALLING A DISHWASHER/WASHING MACHINE

The kitchen is the ideal location for dishwashers and washing machines, not just for the sake of access and convenience, but also because all the necessary plumbing is already in place.

- For dishwashers you will only need a cold water inlet, assuming you're installing a new unit. Most washing machines now only require a cold water inlet too. Check with the manufacturer's instructions.

- In addition to this you will need a waste outlet and a connection to a power source – ideally a socket with an isolator.

- If you are installing the new unit close to a sink, you will need to extend the existing water pipes to the new appliance. Self-cutting supply connectors are the easiest way to cut into the existing supply, but as they are not suitable for all appliances you should again check the manufacturer's instructions.

- Once the water supply is off, the base of the connector is clamped around the water pipe, then the tap screws in to pierce the water pipe. The hose from the washing machine or dishwasher then attaches to this and you're ready to go.

- The alternative to this is to use a T-fitting. Add this as a new junction in the water pipe. T-fittings can be fitted with a stop tap, which isolates the supply to the appliance.

- For the waste pipe you can connect up to the sink drain using a self-cutting waste connector, which works in the same way as the supply connector described above. Alternatively, you can feed the hose directly into a soil pipe if it is close to your appliance.

INSTALLING A TUMBLE DRYER

Where you locate a tumble dryer depends entirely on the type of unit you've bought. A condenser dryer can be placed anywhere in a kitchen or utility room – or indeed any well-ventilated room – though it makes sense to keep it close to the washing machine.

A vented dryer releases moisture through a flexible hose – this can be fixed by drilling a hole through the wall, but most people just prefer to route the hose through an open window. To improve the efficiency of the machine, the distance from the unit to the far end of the hose should be as short as possible.

INSTALLING A COOKER HOOD/ EXTRACTOR FAN

The electrical installation of cooker hoods and extractor fans requires Part P building regulations approval, so contact your local authority in the first instance or use a qualified electrician. You aren't advised to carry out this work yourself unless you have a great deal of experience with electrical installations.

However, to save time and money, you can undertake elements of the installation yourself. Extractor fans and cooker hood extractors suck the air out of the room through a duct drilled into the masonry of an outside wall. The extractor shouldn't be positioned close to a door or window where the vented air will just re-circulate back into the room. Once you've found a suitable position for the vent, you can drill your hole in one of two ways:

1. **Hire a coring bit and heavy-duty drill.** A coring bit is a large-scale drill bit with sharp grinding teeth that will drill out a large hole in masonry in one go. You can get one that will fit the exact size of hole you wish to create. It is a very tough job that requires a steady hand, strength and a powerful drill.

2. **Draw out a template of the hole on the wall.** Using a standard drill and masonry drill bit, drill a series of holes around the perimeter of the larger hole as if you are 'nibbling' away at the larger hole. Then remove the remaining central plug of masonry with a cold chisel and a lump hammer.

Mount the cooker hood onto wall brackets above the cooker and lead the duct pipe to the vent hole. Then get an electrician to connect the hood to the mains circuit.

Pocket tip 🔨

When drilling straight through any substance, always remember to ease off the pressure just before you break through the far side. This will lessen the likelihood of damage, splintering or flaking to the other side.

FITTING A NEW SINK

Step one is to remove your old sink. Be careful when removing any fixed installation – if it's been well fitted, it will be secured to the wall and any rough treatment will bring great lumps of the wall away too. The last thing you need before a major installation job is a major plaster repair job too.

Assuming you're fitting a new sink as part of an overall kitchen installation, you probably have a piece of worktop sitting over your sink unit cut to size with a jigsaw. If not, that's your next step, remembering to check all your measurements carefully before you cut, although most sink manufacturers now helpfully provide a template for you to use when cutting.

Rule of thumb ✌

Attach all the connections to a sink, bath or basin – including the taps – before fixing it into place. It will save you hours of fiddling around in tight corners.

● Attach the new taps to the sink along with the waste pipe and the overflow hose.

- Bond the waste outlet with mastic to waterproof it and ensure all the nuts are tight – this will stop them turning when you come to attach to the water supply.

- Fix the new sink into place on a sealing strip – this should be supplied with the sink – and clip it to the worktop to secure it.

- Then connect the waste outlet to the waste pipe and the taps to the water supply.

FITTING NEW TAPS

If you're just going to replace the taps rather than the whole sink, the job is less complicated but no less awkward. The main problem you'll experience is getting the old taps to budge. You may find it easier to use a basin wrench, which is a special type of spanner designed to give you better leverage in tight spaces. If all else fails, you may need to cut off the connection to the tap below the connector using a hacksaw.

- First, turn off the water supply. Then undo the nut on the tap connector. This is where your basin wrench comes in – you can also use it to undo the back nut on the tap tail.

- Once these two nuts are removed, the tap should come away freely, though you may have to carefully cut away any sealant that's been used around the base of the tap.

- Put the new tap in place and re-install the nuts. You may need to use a short extension pipe if the distance from the tap tail to the tap connector is too short.

⚒ BATHROOM ⚒

INSTALLING A SHAVER SOCKET/POWER SHOWER

Bathrooms are the highest risk areas when it comes to electrical installations. Many experienced DIY experts would not attempt to install shaver sockets and power showers in a bathroom. As the risk of electric shock is so high, you are strongly advised to use a suitably qualified professional.

INSTALLING A BASIN

With the old basin out of the way, you'll need to do as much plumbing work to the new basin as possible prior to attaching it to the wall.

● Turn the new basin upside down and attach the tap connectors and the waste trap.

● Then fix the new taps to the basin and make sure all the nuts are tight.

Pocket tip ⚒

When removing a basin, use a sharp craft knife or razor edge to cut the silicone seal between the basin and the wall. When you come to remove the basin from its fixings, you will do far less damage to the wall.

Connecting the basin to the wall is a two-person job unless you have a pedestal for the basin. If you do, and you're working alone:

- Rest the basin on to the pedestal.

- Check the level and mark the fixing holes for the wall brackets.

- Then remove the basin and pedestal and drill the holes for the bracket.

Make sure you use screws and fixings of an appropriate strength and length to support the basin.

Rule of thumb ✔

Waste from a basin, bath and shower should have a minimum fall of 6mm across every 300mm to the vertical stack. The waste pipe should not be any longer than 3m.

INSTALLING A BATH

As with sinks and basins, fit as much plumbing to the bath as you possibly can prior to installation. You can attach the taps, the over-flow and the waste trap before putting the new bath into position.

Another key factor to consider before fixing the bath into place is support. Does the new bath have feet? Does it come with a cradle to support it? You will need some kind of wooden plank supports to sit under the feet and spread the load over a wider area.

- Place the bath on its wooden supports in position and check levels with your spirit level.

- Adjust the feet to get the levels exactly right.

Pocket tip ↖

Don't worry about making a gravity 'fall' on your bath to drain the water away. It will have been designed to fall down towards the plug hole anyway.

- Once the bath is secured in position and levelled, you can connect it to the waste pipe and water supply.

- Make sure all fittings are secure and then restore the water supply to test for leaks before fixing the bath panel in place.

- Finally, fill the bath with water and apply a seam of silicone between the bath and the wall. This will prevent any water from getting down the crack. The bath is filled with water prior to sealing to ensure the sealant doesn't crack when the bath takes the extra weight of the water (and the bather).

INSTALLING A WC

Most modern toilets are close-coupled designs. Other variations are possible, and different toilets have slightly different methods of installation. The following is a brief guide to installing a close-coupled unit, but you should check the manufacturer's instructions carefully.

- First, push the flexible connector into the soil pipe.

- Then assemble the flush mechanism and secure it inside the cistern.

- Fix the push button assembly to the cistern lid and then add the inlet valve assembly to the cistern. Use the nut to attach this firmly.

- Then place the cistern onto the pan and secure it using connecting bolts and wing nuts – don't overtighten these as you may crack the cistern.

Now you're ready to fix the whole unit to the floor.

- Slide it into place and connect the pan to the flexible waste connector.

- Then drill into the floor to secure the pan.

- The cistern may also need to be fixed to the wall at the back.

- Finally, connect the cold water supply to the cistern.

Pocket tip 🔨

Use rubber washers when fixing toilets and basins to walls and floors – this will protect the ceramic.

INSTALLING A SHOWER UNIT

Types of shower tray vary, so again you will need to consult the manufacturer's instructions carefully as you install, but the following considerations should be taken into account.

- You need enough of a 'fall' beneath the shower tray for the water to drain away into the waste pipe. If there's not enough room, you will need to make a trench in the floor to ensure the waste is carried away.

- Once you've sorted out the waste pipe, you need to secure the shower tray to the floor. If it has feet, turn the tray over and use a spirit level to check that they are even before putting it onto the surface. Secure the feet to the floor if possible.

Otherwise, consider using mortar to seal in the base so that it is strong enough to take the weight.

- Next, check that all the other elements of the job are complete – is the shower area tiled? Is the pipe work and (unconnected) cabling for the shower accessible? If not, get these areas sorted before you build the enclosure.

- Next erect the enclosure according to the manufacturer's instructions. You will need to attach the enclosure to your recently tiled bathroom wall. To do this successfully without breaking any tiles, place masking tape over the tile, mark out the hole onto the masking tape and leave the tape in place as you gently drill through with a tile drill bit. Don't put excessive pressure on the drill as you push through. Go through the tile and into the wall.

- Screw the enclosure in place.

- When the enclosure is finished, use silicone sealant along any joints between the cubicle, tray and the tiled walls.

> 'It takes half of your life before you discover life is a do-it-yourself project.'
> *Napoleon Hill*

⟤ OUTDOORS ⟢

FITTING A NEW TV OR RADIO AERIAL

Attaching an aerial to a roof is a dangerous job because of the height involved combined with the weight and awkwardness of the aerial you're carrying. If you're keen to save money by installing your own aerial, you could try fixing the aerial to a joist in your loft, especially if you're in an area close to a transmitter. While loft-based aerials don't have the same power as exterior ones, they have the massive advantage of being safer to install.

However, if you are keen to get up your ladder, *don't* be tempted to climb onto the roof itself to install the aerial. Instead, attach it to a metal bracket that's securely fixed to the wall of the house.

Pocket tip ↖

To get the best signal, follow the direction of your neighbours' antennae.

FITTING AN OUTDOOR TAP

The best place for an outdoor tap is running straight from the kitchen sink or a similar suitable cold water tap – for example, in the downstairs toilet or utility room. You can buy specially pre-pared kits that include all the equipment you need, but this is a fairly straightforward plumbing job and you might want to try it out to build up your skills.

- First, turn off the water supply.

- Cut into the water supply pipe using a plumber's pipe cutter.

- Compression fit a T-piece into the pipe and next fit an isolating valve.

- Then run the pipe to a convenient place in the wall where you can drill through.

- Run the pipe through the wall – reinforcing the hole if necessary to protect the copper pipe – and then through a 90-degree bend up to a suitable height.

- Secure the pipe to the outside wall using brackets. Then attach a back plate for the tap at the top of the pipe and screw the tap fitting into this plate.

- Switch on the water again and you're ready to go.

INSTALLING GUTTERING

Replacing broken plastic guttering or old-style cast iron guttering is a relatively straightforward process if you have the right kit for the job and a safe and secure ladder to work from.

Rule of thumb ✔

There are two standard types of gutter:

- *For houses, use 112mm gutters with 68mm down pipes.*
- *For sheds, greenhouses and outbuildings, use 75mm gutters and 50mm down pipes.*

Work out the dimensions of the area to be replaced – and thus the length of guttering required – and the number of brackets you will need to fix the new guttering securely. You should use a fascia bracket every metre or so.

Remove the old guttering, taking extra care with heavy sections if you're off balance at the top of a ladder. Remove the old gutter brackets even if they seem to be in reasonably good condition. They will almost certainly perish faster than the new brackets you are installing and this could damage your new gutter.

- First, fit an outlet directly over a drain. Use a plumb line to test it is straight or, if you're working on a still day, simply pour some water through it. Secure this outlet to the fascia.

Rule of thumb ✔

Outlets should be set lower than the far end of the gutter. Make sure there's a 10mm drop across every 6 metres of guttering.

- Fix the fascia brackets, working in a straight line from the farthest point to the outlet. Use a piece of string to guide you.

- Then fit the main guttering, joining pieces together with a union clip.

- At the end of the gutter run, either fit a stop end or, if you're working round a corner, fit an angle piece.

- Secure the down pipe to the outlet and then attach it to the wall using a socket pipe clip at the top and then at intervals of 1.8m.

- At the bottom, if the down pipe is discharging into a gully, fit a down pipe shoe (a curved end pipe) and secure this to the wall with another pipe clip.

Pocket tip 🔨

While you're up the ladder installing your new guttering, fit leaf guards over down pipes and other areas of guttering that are likely to become blocked with leaves.

FITTING A WATER BUTT

Step one in fitting a water butt is finding the most convenient down pipe to divert. You need a good firm base for the butt and its stand – you can use breeze blocks as a stand if you don't want to spend extra on a plastic base. Just remember that the butt needs to be steady and there needs to be enough space underneath the tap for a watering can.

- Mark the height of the water butt on the down pipe, then move down 40mm–50mm and cut the drain with a hacksaw.

- Fit a rain diverter and measure across from this to the water butt.

- Cut a hole in the water butt for the rain diverter.

- Put the lid on the butt, if supplied, and wait for the rain.

OUTDOOR POWER AND LIGHTS

Outdoor power and lighting must have Part P building regulations approval. Don't attempt any outside installations yourself unless you are extremely experienced and you have notified the local authority of the work you are doing.

The safer option

You can run pre-assembled low-voltage garden lighting kits from an indoor socket, via a transformer, through cable that runs out of your house – normally through a hole drilled in a door or window frame – which can then be safely buried through your garden to the lights. Low-voltage lighting kits are normally mounted on spikes and run in a chain, so you can have around four lights connected from the same plug.

Q How do Eskimos stop rain getting in through their front door?
A Weather seals.

⚡ KEEN TO GO GREEN . . . ⚡

If you're planning a major upgrade of your kitchen and bathroom, it's also a good time to consider 'green' alternatives that can cut your water and energy consumption and save you money into the bargain. Here are some eco-friendly ideas:

- Installing a low-flow showerhead can save up to half the water and energy used in a typical shower.

- Make sure you fit a dual-flush toilet in the bathroom – they use up to 30% less water than single flush varieties.

- Use tile or stone floors in the kitchen and bathroom rather than vinyl – the construction method of vinyl uses far more energy than other, more natural flooring solutions.

- When replacing taps, consider low-flow alternatives, or fit aerator heads to existing taps to cut water consumption.

- Get a cistern displacement device from your local water company to reduce the amount of water used when flushing the toilet. Or simply fill a plastic one-litre bottle with water and leave it in the cistern. Don't use a brick, however, as this will disintegrate and will ultimately damage your toilet.

Did you know?
Home accident statistics show that 28% of all accidents happen in the spring months and on Saturday and Sunday afternoons, so be extra careful!

KEEN TO SAVE MONEY . . .

DIY projects can save the earth, but they don't need to cost the earth. Budget DIY is increasingly popular, as people seek to maximise their return on a property investment while ensuring a good-quality finish. Some of the best tips include:

- If you want to brighten up a room but can't afford to completely redecorate, try painting one wall in a very striking shade. Chimney breasts are always great 'feature' walls for a splash of bold colour.
- A new lighting scheme, pictures and plants are all cost-effective ways to change the look of a room.
- Adding 'period' features to your home, such as coving, dados and picture rails, can add great visual impact at minimal expense.
- Try out colour schemes by painting picture frames or mirror frames in a bold shade. If you grow to love it, splash out on a whole wall!

4

KNOW YOUR TRADES

Part of the pleasure of DIY is the knowledge that you're using a skill that is saving you money – that you're remaining independent from the costly and trouble-prone process of employing a contractor. But we all have our limits and need to know when to call in extra help to assist with a major job. This is especially true for specialist work – gas and electricity, plastering and rendering – and for major structural work such as building.

Just because a job is beyond your individual capabilities doesn't mean you shouldn't get involved. There are two reasons to develop 'insider' knowledge of major DIY projects:

- First, there may be essential and time-consuming (ie expensive) groundwork that you can do which will help to keep the budget low.

- Second, you need sufficient awareness of the job to ensure your chosen contractor is doing the job in the right way – and not taking liberties with your cash.

So this chapter gives you an outline of best practice in a range of key trades, as well as guidance on sourcing the best materials (another potential cost saving on a project) and a list of the essential tools of each trade. It also gives advice on how to get the most from the contractor.

⊷ SIZE IT UP RIGHT ⊷

The length, width, weight and diameter of most DIY materials are calculated using the metric scale. Lengths are given in metres or millimetres (1,000mm to a metre). They are rarely measured in centimetres as this can cause confusion. However, many DIY enthusiasts (and shops for that matter) still use the UK imperial scale. So to avoid confusion when measuring out a job, here's a basic guide to the key conversions between the metric and imperial scales of measurement:

Imperial	Metric	Metric	Imperial
1 inch	25.4mm	10 millimetres	0.39in
1 foot	304.8mm	1 metre	3.28ft
1 yard	0.91m	1 metre	1.09 yards
1 square inch	64.5sq mm	10 square millimetres	0.16in
1 square yard	0.84sq m	1 square metre	1.2sq yards
1 acre	0.4 hectares	1 hectare	2.47 acres
1 pint	568.3ml	1 litre	1.76 pints
1 gallon	4.55 litres	1 litre	0.22 gallon
1 ounce	28.35g	1 gram	0.035 ounces
1 pound	0.45kg	1 kilogram	2.21 pounds

'Plan well before you take the journey. Remember the carpenter's rule: Measure twice, cut once.'
Author unknown

⊶ WOODWORKING ⊶

BEST PRACTICE

DIY Golden Rule No. 3 ✎
Measure twice, cut once.

Rule number one of woodworking is to think ahead; don't start any carpentry without knowing what you're doing, as the potential for waste is huge. For example, if you're cutting out a lock on a door, be aware that when chiselling out an edge, you can split the door by applying too much pressure at a critical point. Switch to a craft knife to score finer lines. Here are some other key points of good woodworking practice:

- Always have a plan of what you are making.

- Use standard timber sizes – lengths come in multiples of 300mm.

- Always work on a firm surface with the timber secured.

- For most DIY jobs, a small tenon saw is likely to be adequate.

- Always keep your hands behind cutting edges.

- Sharp tools are easier and safer to use than blunt ones.

- When screwing into wood, always drill a pilot hole.

- When nailing near the edge of timber, drill a pilot hole.

- For marking out timber, use a set square.

- If you're planing a door, always work towards the inside; don't run a plane to the outside corner as it will break out.

TOOLKIT

In addition to the basic toolkit outlined in Chapter 1 – a carpenter's tool bag should include the following:

- **A tool-belt** – preferably a light cloth belt that can be used to hold hammers, screwdrivers and chisels safely.

- **A steel rule** – for accurate measurement and marking out.

- **G-clamps** – to hold wood securely in place while cutting, planing and shaping.

- **Mole-grips** – a special type of pliers that locks onto an object, leaving your hands free.

- **Bradawl** – useful for making small holes in an object – useful for starting off screws.

- **Pliers** – for bending and cutting wire.

- **Pincers** – for removing nails and tacks.

- **Shaping tool** – works like a rasp to shape and contour wood.

- **Plane** – for taking layers of wood from a door, window, etc, and creating a smooth finish.

- Various grades of **sandpaper** – for smoothing wood finish. Fine-grade sandpaper can also be used to take the edge off plasterboard.

- **Nail punch** – a solid metal tool that allows you to flatten nails against the wood without leaving unsightly hammer head marks.

Electrical tools to hire (or buy, if you plan on frequent use):

- **Router** – a hand tool that creates moulded edging and grooves in wood.

- **Belt/disc sander** – a powerful sanding device that's perfect for stripping floors or doors prior to staining or varnishing.

- **Jigsaw/circular saw** – a jigsaw is a useful tool for cutting curves and shapes in wood and man-made boards. Circular saws are heavy-duty machines that are used to accurately cut large or thick lengths of timber.

Pocket tip ↖

Rather than hiring a circular saw, mark up the necessary cuts on the timber you buy from the builders' merchant or DIY warehouse and get them to do the major cuts for you – most will offer a cutting service and it'll save you a great deal of time and effort.

FIXINGS

The fixings you choose depend, not surprisingly, on the type of work you're doing and how neat and/or strong you want the finish to be. Over the course of the projects outlined in this book, a variety of fixings have been recommended – from heavyweight nails such as decking brads, which are perfect for a once-only fix of timber to timber, to screws mounted with rubber washers to safely secure ceramic bathroom accessories, to adhesives that fix delicate mitre-cut dado rails together. There's no simple prescription for what you should use and when, but here's a guide to the basic alternatives available:

Nails

Best for fixing wood to wood or masonry. There are four common types of nail:

- Oval-head nails, which are best for detailed joinery work.

- Lost-head nails, which are good for attaching panelling to timber frames.

- Round-head nails, which are good for general joinery work.

- Masonry nails for fixing timber to masonry.

The size of nails is given in millimetres.

Screws

The two main types are cross-head (sometimes called Phillips head) and slotted-head.

- Cross-head screws are better driving screws if you want something to be really secure or if you're planning to use an electric screwdriver.

- Screw heads are either raised, flush (flat against the surface) or concealed. If you're not planning to remove the screw and you want to conceal a joint, you can cover it with wood filler.

The length of screws is given in both imperial and metric measurements, while the diameter of the screw is given as a number (or gauge). The bigger the number, the bigger the screw.

Pocket tip ↖

To give a screw a firmer drive into wood, tip it with PVA or a drop of oil-based paint.

Secure fixings

When you're attaching something heavy to a weaker surface – such as a basin to plasterboard, or shelving to timber frame – you'll need to secure the fixing with a **wall plug**. Most are plastic plugs that hold the screw firm – make sure you choose the right size plug to match with the screw; details are given on the packaging.

For a tougher job, you can use metal plasterboard plugs or spring toggles, which pop open to form a non-return base when they are pushed through a hole in plasterboard.

Pocket tip ↖

WD40, or equivalent, is a great spray solution for the treatment of squeaks, stiff nuts and other plumbing problems. But it is also excellent for putting on screws if you're screwing into difficult surfaces, as it helps them to glide in nicely. The same is true for soap – just a small amount on the head of a screw will help you grip more effectively.

Adhesives

These are becoming increasingly sophisticated and are now a popular alternative to nails in many applications. There's more information on adhesives on pp. 146–7.

MATERIALS

Most of the timber that you'll use for everyday DIY jobs can be sourced from DIY stores. But if you're ordering in bulk or are looking for particularly high-quality or unusual wood, go to a specialist timber merchant. A great way to find out where and how to source specialist materials is to go onto online blogs and chatrooms (see internet resources on pp. 166–8).

Rule of thumb ✔

Remember that softwood timber sizes given at the timber merchants relate to sawn sizes, not finished sizes, ie 50mm × 25mm timber planed all round (PAR) ends up 45mm × 20mm after planing.

Timber is sold in multiples of 300mm, so bear this in mind when you're measuring up for a job. Try to source all your timber at the same time and from the same place; this will ensure an even quality of finish. Check each piece of timber carefully for bowing, warping, split ends and dead knots.

Pocket tip 🔨

If you're trying to source authentic or period features for a house renovation, go to an architectural salvage yard. Prices and quality vary, but you can often get a good deal on old brick, roofing tiles, floor tiles and ironmongery. To source individual items without leaving the comfort of your own home, visit salvage website www.salvo.co.uk

FINDING HELP – CARPENTERS

Unlike electricians and plumbers, there's no single industry body that defines best practice for a carpenter, so if you do want to get help, how do you ensure quality craftsmanship?

Most people are happy to get a referral, but going on word of mouth can be a risk, even if the recommendation comes from someone you trust. That doesn't mean their definition of quality workmanship and yours are the same.

You're well within your rights to ask to see some of the carpenter's previous work. If someone has recommended them, have a look at that person's job. Seeing how well a door has been hung, or how well the hinges have been cut into the door, can tell you more than a hundred referrals. Take a look at the materials used, check the fit and finish, and see how the doors shut.

All of these details will tell you whether you're employing someone with the right level of skill for your job.

Q Which part of the government is made of MDF?
A The cabinet.

⊱ ELECTRICS ⊰

BEST PRACTICE

Electrical best practice is all about working safely within your comfort zone. If you are unsure about any electrical work, you should never attempt to do it on your own. The following standard rules apply in any circumstance.

- Switch off the power before you begin any electrical work.

- Always use three-core flex when an earth connection is required.

- Never touch an electrical appliance with wet hands or position an electrical appliance in a wet area such as a bathroom.

- Don't overload lighting circuits – you shouldn't wire more than 12 lights to a single circuit. The ideal number is around eight.

- When you're working on a circuit, always remove the relevant MCB or fuse block from the consumer unit/fuse box and stick it in your pocket after you've switched off the power. This will ensure that no one accidentally switches everything back on while you're working.

- Use the right tools for the job.

TOOLKIT

For basic electrical work, you will need the following tools:

- cable locator

- wire cutters/strippers

- electrical screwdriver

- circuit tester

- spare fuses and fuse wire (if required)

- good quality torch (ideally a halogen head torch)
- green and yellow PVC earth insulating sleeve
- pliers.

MATERIALS

DIY stores can be expensive for electrical accessories such as cabling, fittings and cable conduits. You can often get a better deal at specialist electrical suppliers (such as Maplin and Screwfix) or from smaller electrical hardware stores.

FINDING HELP – ELECTRICIANS

As outlined above, the definition of a competent electrician is quite specific in terms of meeting the requirements of local authority building control regulations. So much electrical work in the home now comes under this remit, so you're well advised to employ an electrician who meets this standard. The following organisations offer training schemes for electricians who wish to become a registered authorised competent person:

Name	Contact number and website
NICEIC Certification Services Ltd	08000 130900 www.niceic.org.uk
ELECSA Ltd	0870 749 0080 www.elecsa.org.uk
British Standards Institution	01442 230442 www.bsi-global.com
BRE Certification Ltd	0870 609 6093 www.partp.co.uk
NAPIT Certification Ltd	0870 444 1392 www.napit.org.uk

An electrician who is certified under schemes run by any of the above will be able to undertake any electrical installation work and will ensure that the work fully complies with building regulations on your behalf. Check the website of any of these training bodies for a list of qualified electricians in your area.

⚒ PLUMBING ⚒

BEST PRACTICE

While complex installations and gas work should be left to the professionals, plumbing is an area where you can slowly build up skills, tools and confidence to a decent level of competence. Start small and build up to major jobs.

Compression or push fittings make the process of connecting up pipe work much simpler than in the old days of soldered copper pipes, but be wary of overusing plastic fittings. While plastic can be very flexible, in hard-to-reach places such as the bath, plastic fittings are not so suitable. With heavy use, the nut connecting to the tap can often loosen, which creates a leak. Unless you have easy access to the pipe work, this will probably lead to you removing the bath to fix the fault.

Another downside of plastic pipes is that they leave you open to rodent attack. If you're running these pipes in your cellar or loft and you've got anything nibbling away in these hard-to-access spaces, you could end up with a nasty leak. It's often better practice to spend the extra on copper pipes. You can still get push fittings that make installation straightforward, but you also have the comfort of knowing that the pipe work is much stronger and more stable.

Pocket tip ✎

Soak new washers in hot water to make them more pliable and easier to use. When fitting new washers or removing a stubborn washer, silicone grease will help the washer slide on and off.

TOOLKIT

For basic plumbing repairs and installations, you will need the following:

- copper pipe cutter
- adjustable wrench
- junior hacksaw
- PTFE tape
- ball valve and tap washers
- radiator bleed key
- sink plunger
- drain rods
- silicone lubricant.

MATERIALS

As with electrical supplies, plumbing supplies can be cheaper and higher quality if they are bought from a specialist store (such as Screwfix or Plumb Centre). With a specialist trade store, you may also find that you get plenty of extra advice for free too!

FINDING HELP – PLUMBERS

Assuming you're tackling basic repairs and emergencies yourself, there are only two alternative circumstances in which you'd need to hire specialist help – if you've got a major installation job that you don't think you can manage alone or if you've got gas work.

As with carpenters, you can tell a lot about a plumber by the standard of the finish, so try to get a referral from a friend who has had work carried out and check the quality of the finish.

- Is the pipe work neat and discreet?

- If the plumber has soldered the pipes, is it a neat job?

- Is the installation neatly finished with silicone sealant and watertight?

- Has the plumber been called back to remedy any faults or leaks in his pipe work?

The more impressive the appearance of your friend's job, the more confidence you can have in the plumber.

Pocket tip ✎

If you can't get a referral, ask at a technical college in your area that trains plumbers. They will have records of qualified tradespeople and may be willing to put you in touch with a former student.

Most plumbers will provide materials. Check out what they are charging for materials and cross-reference it with an online DIY store. If their costs seem high, see if the plumber will be happy to work with materials you have sourced yourself.

As plumbers often charge by the hour, you should work out what you want done in advance and discuss the scope of works in detail before the plumber begins. Don't give your plumber the opportunity to 'gold-plate' the job by taking too long over the installation. You could even negotiate a time-based schedule of works before the job starts.

> *Rule of thumb* ✎
>
> *A plumber should charge no more than about £50 for a call-out and £30–£40 per hour for work done. Anything vastly in excess of this figure is out of the ordinary and should be queried. Always get at least three quotes, even if you're going to use a plumber on referral – if the plumber knows they are in a competitive bidding process, they will give you a better price.*

GAS WORK

This type of work should always be left to a qualified professional. From April 2009, the register of competent gas engineers changed from the CORGI gas registration scheme to the Gas Safe Register. Under this scheme each qualified engineer is given an ID card with a unique licence number, which tells you exactly what type of work they are permitted to do.

The Gas Safe Register allows you to enter the engineer's licence number onto its website to double check the skills and authenticity of the gas engineer you are employing. For more details, and to find a qualified engineer in your area, visit www.gassaferegister.co.uk or call the helpline on 0800 408 5500.

'If I had my life to live over again, I'd be a plumber.
Albert Einstein

⊱ PAINTING AND DECORATING ⊰

BEST PRACTICE

This is probably the area of DIY that people are most confident tackling without outside help – although there are certain circumstances in which you should consider employing a professional (see below). Generally, decorating is an accessible and enjoyable art of the DIY process. Make sure you follow these essential guidelines:

- Preparation is everything. The quality of your finish is entirely dependent on the quality of your preparation.

- Remove any loose and flaky material from the surface you're working on.

- Where possible, use water-based paints. It is easier to clean brushes and spills, and you don't breathe in so many harmful additives.

- One-coat paints sound like a great idea, but they will only work in certain circumstances – such as over a very well-prepared, light base.

- Non-drip gloss. Non-drip means it won't come off the brush, but it doesn't mean it won't run if you slop it on. You have to be quite strong to apply non-drip gloss, especially in cool weather, as it is a very viscous substance and it's hard to produce a consistent finish. It can sometimes be better to apply several coats of a thinner product.

- Avoid leaving brush strokes when applying emulsion to a wall by using a fine-piled quality roller.

- Most paints are a bit thick, so thin the paint slightly and this will help you avoid a stippled orange-peel effect when the paint is dry.

- For a fine finish, use a fine roller.

Pocket tip ✦

When you mark up a wall for a screw hole, don't mark it with a single dot, as this will be lost the moment you start drilling. Use a cross (+) which will allow you to identify whether the bit is moving as you drill.

If you've been sanding, filing or doing anything which produces a very fine dust spray the area with a mist of water before you start cleaning it up, this will make the particles of dust stick together and will speed up your job.

TOOLKIT

Brushes

Good brushes that are well treated last a lifetime. Don't waste your money on cheap brushes that will lose bristles unless you're painting a garden fence or brickwork, in which case they'll do the job perfectly well. It's worth investing in a whole set of brushes, including extra small, angled, fine-detail brushes. These are perfect for architrave and door frames.

Pocket tip ↖

To preserve paint brushes for longer, wash them thoroughly to remove any trace of paint residue and then wrap them in kitchen towel, sealing the towel with an elastic band. Then allow them to dry naturally.

Rollers

The quality of the roller will have an impact on the quality of the finish, but all reasonable rollers should give you a nice even spread of paint. Don't forget to clean the roller with masking tape or parcel tape before using it for the first time. For awkward spots, such as down the backs of radiators, use a special long-handled roller.

Pads and other methods

To get an ultra-even finish, hire a high-volume low-pressure sprayer. They work like a reverse vacuum cleaner. They take a litre of paint or so and will cover huge areas very quickly, which is a great way to paint things such as detailed cast iron radiators or fancy panelled doors.

You will also need:

- **Masking tape** – to protect surfaces that are not to be painted.

- **A paint kettle** – to store a small amount of paint at a time – thus minimising contamination from grit and dust in the remaining paint.

- **Sandpaper and scrapers** – to prepare surfaces prior to painting.

MATERIALS

> ### Rule of thumb ✔
>
> *One litre of emulsion or primer covers around 10sq m of wall. The same volume of gloss covers around 15sq m.*

Types of paint

There is a huge variety of paint types on the market. The main ones are given below:

Type of paint	Usage	Finish	Notes	Cleaning
Oil-based				
Primer	Wood/metal	Flat	To seal bare wood	White spirit
Undercoat	Wood/metal/ plaster	Semi-flat	Base for top coat	White spirit
Gloss	Wood/metal/ plastic	High sheen	Hardwearing/ durable	White spirit
Eggshell	Wood	Satin	Hardwearing/ durable	White spirit
Water-based				
Primer	Wood/metal	Flat	Use on interior wood	Water/soap
Undercoat	Wood/metal/ plaster	Semi-flat	Base for water-based top coat	Water/soap
Satin	Wood/metal/ plaster	Mid sheen	Durable	Water/soap
Eggshell	Wood/metal/ plaster	Mid sheen	Interior top coat	Water/soap
Vinyl matt emulsion	Plaster	Flat	General purpose	Water/soap

Type of paint	Usage	Finish	Notes	Cleaning
Vinyl silk emulsion	Plaster	Mid sheen	General purpose	Water/soap
Others				
Varnish	Woodwork	Various	Water or oil-based	Check label
Wood stain	Woodwork	Matt/silk	As above	Check label
Knotting fluid	Woodwork	Matt/silk	Sealant for knots prior to painting/ varnishing or staining	White spirit

In addition, there is specialist paint for metal – including radiators as well as interior and exterior metalwork.

Pocket tip 🔨

When you've finished using paint and want to store it for another day, secure the lid tightly then turn the tin upside down for a few seconds before turning it back upright. This allows for an airtight seal to form around the lid so that when you reuse the paint there's no thick skin on top of the tin.

Types of sealant

Sealants are increasingly used in decorating and plumbing to create water-tight finishes. Most are available in cartridge formats, which need to be applied with a sealant gun. This is by far the most cost-effective way to use sealant.

● **Decorating sealant.** This is perfect for filling gaps around window frames, in the gaps between walls and ceiling and to fill hairline cracks.

- **Kitchen and bathroom sealant.** This flexible silicone sealant is used to create watertight seals between units and walls.

- **Gutter and roof sealant.** Another specialist variant, which has a stronger weather-proofing bond that's perfect for roof repairs.

You can also buy expanding foam products, which are useful if you need to fill in a hole – perhaps where a disused piece of pipe work has been removed. These don't provide such a neat finish but you can skim and paint over gaps that have been filled with this substance.

Pocket tip 🔨

Work a screw into the cut-off nozzle of a sealant cartridge when you've finished using it for the day as this will stop a plug of hardened sealant forming.

Types of adhesive

There are many types of adhesive on the market.

- Polyvinyl adhesive (PVA) is perfect for a repair to wood, panelling or veneer or for re-fixing joints in furniture.

- Exterior-grade PVA glue is also available for outdoor working.

- Super glues are used for sticking metal to metal, glass and ceramic.

- An even stronger glue is the epoxy-resin glue, consisting of a two-part kit that works together to form an incredibly strong bond. This will bond metal to metal, providing an extremely strong result.

Rule of thumb ❦

When using super glues and epoxy-resin mixes, care should be taken to avoid contact with skin. Always wear latex gloves, and if you do get your hands near the glue, wipe it off straight away.

You can also buy adhesive in cartridges, which is extremely useful for simple decorating jobs such as securing skirting boards and dado rails to walls. Apply the adhesive to the item you're sticking to the wall and keep pressure on it for a few seconds.

Pocket tip ❦

If you get general purpose adhesive on your hands, rub them in some flour or some dry filler powder. The adhesive will stick to the powder and will peel off your skin more easily.

FINDING HELP – DECORATORS

While you should be confident that you'll be able to manage most decorating jobs yourself, there are a couple of considerations you should bear in mind.

1. **Is the job too dangerous?** Painting exterior woodwork on a ladder or painting ceilings over the stairs or in a high-ceilinged room may be a straightforward job if you're steady on your feet and good with heights. Otherwise, a professional decorator will have the tools and the experience to finish the elements of the job you can't reach.

2. **Is the job too fiddly?** There's no safety issue associated with painting door and window frames, working around architraves, coving and ceiling roses, but there is a time cost and a real impact on the finish of the job if the paintwork is roughly finished. Consider doing the bulk of the decorator's job yourself and then hiring someone for a day to finish off.

Your best source of a good decorator is a previous satisfied customer, and it is also the most likely source of evidence that the decorator can deliver a professional finish.

Q Why do painters get upset so easily?
A Because they're very emulsional.

Q Why was the builder so short?
A Because he had been contracting for a long time.

⚒ BUILDING ⚒

BEST PRACTICE

If you want to tackle a small-scale building job, you still need to be aware of the regulations that exist in your area. What you can build depends on where you live – obviously you can't build onto public land, but even if it's your own land, you should call the local planning authority to check. Conservation areas and listed buildings have their own rules and you should check to see whether you need anyone's permission before you start any building work.

If you're tackling a small-scale job such as building a porch, then providing it's not within 6 feet of your neighbour's property and doesn't enclose a large space, you should be okay. All structures need foundations of hardcore beneath a concrete base. When building any structures attached to your house – as with a porch or conservatory – you are advised to include some insulation. Also remember to put in a damp-proof membrane at the same height as it is on the walls of your house.

TOOLKIT

In addition to the basic tools outlined in Chapter 1, a small-scale building job may well require the following tools:

- lump hammer

- cold chisel

- bolster – a wide-faced chisel used for cutting bricks

- sledgehammer

- trowel

- steel float.

You may also consider hiring the following:

- cement mixer

- paving slab cutter.

MATERIALS

The materials you require will obviously vary from job to job, but you should check with your local council regarding their rules for kerbside deliveries of sand, gravel and other materials. It may be easier and safer to order large tonne bags of raw materials. A builders' merchant is the best starting point.

Pocket tip ✎

Buy sand and cement, hardcore, bricks and other materials in bulk from builders' merchants. You'll get better prices than at the DIY store and plenty of free expert advice into the mix.

FINDING HELP – BUILDERS

Alongside an electrician, and possibly a plumber, a builder is the professional you are most likely to engage to carry out work on your behalf. The general guidance outlined above for getting real proof of the quality of their work by inspecting previous jobs also holds true for builders. Always be wary of a builder who isn't proud to show you his past jobs.

In addition to this general idea, there are some extra things to consider when commissioning a builder for a big job.

- Work out a clear brief for the job and prepare a detailed outline for prospective bidders. This will show them that you are serious and it will help focus your mind to ensure you don't end up with a costly change of heart mid-project.

- Doing any groundwork/preparation yourself will save you time and money.

- Get at least three quotes from builders and make sure they come out and properly inspect the site of the proposed works. Anyone who seems very relaxed about providing a quote is only behaving that way because they expect the prices to skyrocket.

- Guard against spiralling costs with your chosen builder by getting them to sign a contract for a fixed-price job. If you agree all costs of labour and materials in advance, the builder cannot come back to you for more money. Try to negotiate penalty clauses for over-running work as well to keep the builder on schedule.

- Check and verify any professional associations that the builder claims to be linked with. Sometimes builders still 'trade off' the name of a reputable industry body even if their own membership of that body has lapsed.

- Agree terms and times of payment. Don't pay the builder in cash, even if you are offered a discount to do so. If the builder is not putting work through the books, this suggests an unscrupulous nature that could just as easily work against you too.

- Have regular meetings with the builder you choose, to make sure they are still on track and have them take the time to explain anything you don't understand. Good channels of communication are essential when managing a major build.

- Make sure you know what the builder needs in terms of access to services — water and electricity in particular.

- Provide the builder with somewhere to make refreshments. Or make them some tea yourself — it's a good way to keep an eye on the job without appearing to be nosy.

Vinegar — the trade's DIY secret

If you thought vinegar was just something that tradesmen put on their lunchtime chips, you're seriously underestimating one of nature's great DIY tools. Vinegar has the following applications around the home:

- *A few drops of vinegar in the mix stops plaster from drying out while you're trying to apply it.*
- *A couple of dishes of vinegar left in a freshly painted room will get rid of nasty odours.*
- *Use a vinegar solution to wash paint from your hands and to remove stubborn, dried paint from brushes.*
- *Apply a vinegar and warm water solution to wallpaper to strip it away easily.*
- *Restore rusty nails, screws and other fixings to full working order by soaking them in vinegar.*

5

DIY SAFETY GUIDE

DIY Golden Rule No. 4 🪜

Always keep a good, well-stocked first aid kit handy. Make sure it contains items such as bandages, eye bath, plasters, surgical tape and gauze as well as some form of antiseptic cream and painkillers.

⊱ GENERAL SAFETY TIPS ⊰

If you consider the fact that a lot of DIY jobs are done under pressure, in bad conditions and with the wrong tools, it's hardly surprising that so many jobs end in disaster. According to the Royal Society for the Prevention of Accidents (RoSPA), more than 200,000 people end up in casualty each year as a direct result of DIY disasters. Some of the more common problems are outlined below, along with some safety guides to keep you from joining the statistics.

> 'Don't force it ... get a bigger hammer.'
> *Arthur Bloch*

Top 10 most common DIY accidents (by project)

1. Woodworking
2. Laying paving/ concrete
3. Nailing
4. Cutting or moving metal bars and sheets
5. Bricklaying
6. Painting
7. Glueing and pasting
8. Screwing
9. Floor and wall tiling
10. Wallpapering

Top 10 most dangerous tools

1. Knives and scalpels (20,000 accidents in the UK each year)
2. Saws (15,000)
3. Grinders (6,500)
4. Hammers (6,000)
5. Chisels (4,000)
6. Screwdrivers (3,500)
7. Power drills (3,000)
8. Axes (2,000)
9. Planes (2,000)
10. Welding equipment (2,000)

(statistics from RoSPA)

⚙ CLOTHING FOR SAFE WORKING ⚙

As well as the essential kit of steel-toed boots and safety goggles, you should also consider kitting yourself out with the following (depending on the type of jobs you tackle):

- **Industrial-strength PVC gloves.** These are good when dealing with chemicals and other harmful substances that shouldn't touch skin – like fast-acting paint strippers. They're also good for dealing with glass or other abrasive materials.

- **Face masks/dust masks.** Absolutely essential kit for dealing with any tasks with airborne fibres or fumes, such as painting or laying insulation.

- **Overalls.** A great way to protect your clothing, but for safety's sake also a good option as there's less loose material to catch in machinery.

- **Ear defenders.** Another essential piece of kit if you're tackling a lot of noisy drilling and cutting jobs.

Did you know?

Over 200,000 people per year are injured while undertaking DIY jobs at home. Figures also show that 30,000 people need hospital treatment each year through ladder-related incidents.

⊶ OTHER HAZARDS ⊷

FUMES

Any job that involves potentially hazardous fumes – such as painting, stripping and tiling – should be carried out in a well-ventilated area. You should never smoke in this area – even if the windows are open.

CARBON MONOXIDE

You shouldn't come into contact with carbon monoxide in the course of DIY as this poisonous gas is caused by problems in a gas fitting. However, if you have had work done, or you have older gas appliances, it may be worth investing in a carbon monoxide alarm. These are free-standing devices similar to smoke alarms that will assess the levels of carbon monoxide in your home and alert you if levels become dangerously high. Simpler colour-changing carbon monoxide detectors are available, but an alarm is the safest option. As with smoke alarms, you must test the battery regularly to make sure it is still working.

ELECTRICITY

Electrical safety is all about taking precautions – switch off the power at the mains before investigating any faults with the wiring circuit and unplug any appliances that appear to be faulty. This is an area where you should not be afraid to seek professional advice. If you are confident enough to do some preliminary investigations of a fault yourself, wear rubber-soled shoes and use the right tools for the job, such as an electrical screwdriver.

Pocket tip 🔨

Keep a chemical fire extinguisher in a handy position in your house. Don't try to use water to put out an electrical fire.

LOCKING AWAY TOOLS

Keep sharp and potentially dangerous tools locked away in a steel tool chest. You should also lock away or store poisons and potentially harmful substances out of reach of children – but don't put them on a high or hard-to-reach shelf; this will just increase the risk of you tipping the chemical over yourself when you next come to use it.

Power tool safety top tips

- *Wear appropriate clothing. This means using a dust mask and ear protection as well as the obligatory eye protection. It's equally important to avoid wearing clothes that are so loose they will catch on saw blades and drill bits.*
- *Unplug the power tool whenever it's not in use. Don't let children or pets anywhere near the tool under any circumstances.*
- *Use a level work surface and ensure that the item you're working on is firmly secured.*
- *Don't work while drunk, tired or under the influence of drugs or medication.*
- *Only use the tools you can confidently handle. A big, powerful hammer drill has a big kick and you must be confident you have the physical strength to manage it*

before you use it. Maintain a firm stance and always ensure you work away from your body.

- *If you're using a wired power tool, ensure you connect it to the mains via an RCD adaptor, as this will reduce the chance of electric shock should you accidentally cut the cable.*
- *The general rule of power tool safety is that you should never apply force to the power tool; you should let it work at its own rate and if you're using a sharp drill bit it will cut in more efficiently. Don't expect it will do the job in one go. Apply gentle pressure little and often and the tool should never sound at all strained.*

LIFTING AND CARRYING

If you're lifting heavy weights, use lifting equipment or enlist the help of several friends. Never take on more than you can handle. It's also very important to assess what you're handling in terms of the working conditions.

Ask yourself whether you've allowed enough space to lift and manoeuvre items without putting unnecessary strain on your back or twisting yourself in such a way as to cause injury.

Even the weather conditions can be a contributing factor – if you're working outside and you've got a large pane of glass or a sheet of plasterboard, a strong wind can turn an otherwise simple job into a potential disaster.

'There are three ways to get something done: do it yourself, hire someone, or forbid your kids to do it.'
Author unknown

✂ USING LADDERS AND
WORKING AT HEIGHTS ✂

One of the main dangers of DIY is working at heights. Ladder safety is incredibly important and you should always work from a level surface. Here are some more key points of ladder sense:

● Extension ladders should be at an angle of 75 degrees to the wall, which is around one step out, four steps up. Many people try to climb ladders at 45 degree angles and find the ladder slips out from under them.

● Always try to work in pairs so that you've got someone footing the ladder. If you can't do that, put a heavy weight at the bottom of the ladder, particularly in places like pre-cast driveways and anywhere that's moss-covered or slippery. Get yourself some big, heavy objects like breeze blocks or a wheelbarrow of sand.

Pocket tip ✎

Before using an extending, detachable loft ladder carefully check the manufacturer's labels attached to the ladder to ensure you're using the right side, as one side is significantly structurally weaker.

● Always wear solid shoes on ladders, and make sure they have good grips.

● Using a ladder stay at the top of the ladder helps. This is a triangular device that keeps you off the wall, so that the ladder creates a larger footprint at the top. It also helps to keep you away from the roofline or gutter.

- Never go beyond the third rung from the top of the ladder — especially if you have nothing to grip in case you slip.

- Carry tools in a belt or fix them to the ladder in a bucket.

- If in doubt, use a safer option — like a scaffolding platform with safety rails.

Better safe than sorry

If you're a committed DIY enthusiast, then no matter how careful and sensible you are, you will have an emergency at some stage. Prepare yourself in advance by taking one of the St John Ambulance's excellent emergency and first aid courses. They are extremely comprehensive and great value for money. Find out more information at www.sja.org.uk.

You know you're a DIY expert when...

1. The Wickes mini catalogue becomes a permanent fixture next to the toilet.

2. You spend hours in work using Word to sketch out the DIY job for that weekend.

3. You have 7 tins of WD-40 in convenient locations around the house.

4. You buy things that you don't need but will look good in the toolbox.

5. You know all of the different shades of white.

6. You have a tool belt.

7. You know that rubbing a graphite pencil on a hinge will stop the squeak.

8. You think you don't need a spirit level. You do.

9. You have a large collection of wood in the shed, just in case.

10. Complete renovation of a cow shed doesn't faze you.

11. You have a compost bin.

12. You have a tape measure in your car.

13. You stop to appreciate your handywork at least once a day.

14. Your work is never done.

15. You can unscrew a screw with a hammer.

GLOSSARY

The following is a brief guide to some of the terms, tools and techniques discussed in the book.

Adjustable spanner – a spanner with a movable jaw that can be sized to fit a range of nuts.

Architrave – the decorative wooden panelling around a door frame.

Basin wrench – a special long wrench that is designed to work in awkward spaces.

Bolster – a flat chisel-like cutting tool used for halving bricks.

Bradawl – a sharp-pointed tool similar to a screwdriver that is used for starting holes in wood.

Building regulations – a series of controls relating to specific areas of house construction and repair. Administered by local authorities around the UK.

Cable locator – a battery-powered device that detects the presence of cables in a wall.

Cavity wall – a wall constructed from two courses of bricks with a gap (cavity) between.

Cold chisel – a large heavy-duty chisel used for hacking masonry.

Compression joint – a push fitting used to attach pieces of pipe work.

Conduit – a plastic or metal box-like sheath that protects electric cables.

Consumer unit – the main fuse box of the house.

Coving – a decorative wood, plaster or polystyrene trim used between the top of the wall and the ceiling.

Craft knife – a sharp, disposable-bladed knife used for fine detail cutting in wood and other household cutting.

Dado rail – a decorative rail of wood that runs around a wall at a height of approximately 1 metre.

Damp-proof membrane – a layer of protective sheet that lessens the likelihood of damp penetration from the ground.

Emulsion – a water-based paint ideal for covering large areas.

Fascia – the name given to the boards that the gutter brackets are attached to under the eaves of the house.

Fungicide – a chemical substance that fights the build-up of mould.

Fuse – an old-fashioned form of protection against overloading or fault on an electrical circuit. Fuses are either simple bare wires stretched between two terminals or cartridges.

Grout – the filler that goes into the spaces between tiles.

Hardcore – a mixture of stone and rubble used as the base layer for concrete foundations.

Junction box – the housing for cable connections, normally between parts of an extended wiring circuit.

MCB – miniature circuit breakers – the modern-day equivalent of fuses, found in a consumer unit.

Mitre box – a special woodworking tool, used in conjunction with a saw to create perfect 45 degree angles in wood.

Nail punch – a metal device that is used to force the heads of nails flush with the surface of wood.

Paint kettle – a small, fixed-handle paint pot that carries small amounts of paint at a time.

Part P regulations – a new major element of building regulations, limiting the amount of electrical installation work that can be undertaken by non-registered people.

Plasterboard – smooth sheets of plaster sealed between thick paper layers.

Plumb line – a weight attached to a line used for measuring vertical drops.

Primer – the first coat applied when painting.

PTFE tape – a strong, white tape used to seal joints in plumbing.

PVA – polyvinyl adhesive – a general all-purpose glue used to attach wood and as a sealant in diluted form.

PVC sleeve – a green and yellow sleeve used to protect and identify earth cabling.

RCD – residual current device – this is a safety device included in modern consumer units that cuts off the power when there's a major fault. Essential to minimise the risk of electric shock.

Render – a sand and cement mix plaster applied to the outside of the house.

Reveal – the hole in a wall in which a window frame is mounted.

Sealant – a flexible compound that creates a watertight seal between kitchen units/bathroom fittings and the wall.

Skim – a thin coat of plaster used to create a smooth finish on a wall.

Soil pipe – the main vertical waste pipe in a property.

Stop cock/stop valve – an isolator valve for the water supply, normally found under the kitchen sink or in the road outside.

Tenon saw – the most versatile cutting saw in the woodworker's toolbox.

Undercoat – the first coat applied when painting.

USEFUL RESOURCES

The internet has many qualities, not least of which is that it offers the perfect forum for people with an incredible amount of knowledge and a keenness to share it. This is obviously a double-edged sword, as some of the information may be incorrect. But as a general rule, you can find plenty of answers to common questions online and it's certainly a good place to look if you want reassurance regarding a specific project.

The following is by no means an exhaustive list of DIY sites – there are hundreds of thousands out there. But this is a pretty good cross-section of what the internet has to offer. Always double check what you read online.

⚒ RECOMMENDED WEBSITES ⚒

www.diydoctor.org.uk
A source of free information for anyone looking to self-build, renovate, remodel, convert or extend. There's also a useful forum where you can post questions.

www.egenie.co.uk
The place to go if you want to search for the best price from a tradesman. Post a free ad with details of your job and tradespeople will bid to do the work.

www.problemsolved.co.uk
Allows you to find, compare and write a review about local trades-people in your area, so that you can share experiences and find a reliable person for the job.

www.ratedpeople.com
Gives you the chance to pick and choose from up to three trades-people for every job you post and it has a ratings system once the job has been done.

www.myhammer.co.uk
Gets you multiple quotes, which means you can hunt around for the most competitive price.

www.home-jane.co.uk
Puts you in touch with professional tradeswomen with all of the skills needed to solve your DIY challenges.

www.consumerprotectionagency.co.uk
A community of independent small to medium sized businesses, which is dedicated to quality workmanship and protects customers from employing rogue traders.

www.badlyratedtradesmen.co.uk
Allows you to search their extensive database of cowboy workmen and black-listed builders for a small joining fee of £2.95.

STORE-SPECIFIC WEBSITES

www.homebase.co.uk

www.wickes.co.uk

www.diy.co.uk (B&Q)

✂ GENERAL INTEREST WEBSITES ✂

www.doityourself.com

www.diynetwork.co.uk

www.diyfixit.co.uk

INDEX

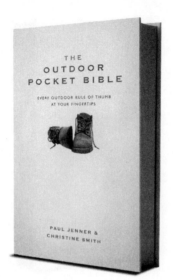

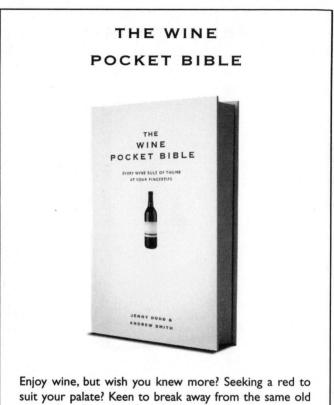